ANSWERS TO
QUESTIONS
MOST
FREQUENTLY
ASKED ABOUT
ORGANIZATION
DEVELOPMENT

ANSWERS TO QUESTIONS MOST FREQUENTLY ASKED ABOUT ORGANIZATION DEVELOPMENT

PHILIP G. HANSON
BERNARD LUBIN

SAGE Publications
International Educational and Professional Publisher
Thousand Oaks   London   New Delhi

For information address:

SAGE Publications, Inc.
2455 Teller Road
Thousand Oaks, California 91320
E-mail: order@sagepub.com

SAGE Publications Ltd.
6 Bonhill Street
London EC2A 4PU
United Kingdom

SAGE Publications India Pvt. Ltd.
M-32 Market
Greater Kailash I
New Delhi 110 048 India

Printed in the United States of America

Library of Congress Cataloging-in-Publication Data

Hanson, Philip G., Ph.D.
    Answers to questions most frequently asked about
organization development / Philip G. Hanson, Bernard Lubin.
        p. cm.
    Includes bibliographical references.
    ISBN 0-8039-5203-1 (c : alk. paper). — ISBN 0-8039-5204-X (p:
alk. paper).
    1. Organizational change—Management. I. Lubin, Bernard, 1923-
HD58.8.H3636   1995
658.4'06—dc20   95-15783

Printed on acid-free paper.

95 96 97 98 99 10 9 8 7 6 5 4 3 2 1

Sage Production Editor: Diane S. Foster

Contents

Foreword

Phil Hanson and Bernie Lubin have provided a much-needed service by developing this volume on organization development. I believe that there has long been a need for an uncomplicated orientation to the field that would invite the reader's thoughtful exploration of concepts, terms, and applications. The authors have drawn on their extensive experience in the organization development field to produce a monograph of broad scope that is also easy to read. The question-and-answer format frames the question or issue and then provides a straightforward response. Unlike some presentations that seem to promise successful organizational change regardless of the situation, the authors do not avoid discussion of the problems and difficulties inherent in what has developed into a very interesting and useful set of concepts and strategies over the past three decades. This book should be of use to managers and graduate students for orientation, terminology, and concepts. It should also be useful to OD consultants as an indication of those areas about which managers need clarification and possible training.

WILLIAM B. EDDY, PH.D.
Dean, Bloch School of Business
and Public Administration
University of Missouri at Kansas City

Acknowledgments

We wish to express our appreciation and to acknowledge Robin W. Hanson for her patience and untiring efforts to produce a final draft of this manuscript. This effort included retyping rough drafts and making many revisions and corrections. During this time she was willing to put many of her own needs on hold until we met our deadline. Thank you again.

We also gratefully acknowledge permission to reprint material from the following sources:

Blank, Renee, & Slipp, Sandra, *Voices of Diversity*, ©1994 by Renee Blank and Sandra Slipp. Published by AMACOM, a division of the American Management Association. All rights reserved. Excerpts are reprinted in Chapter 5 with permission of the publisher.

Burke, W. Warner, *Organizational Development: A Process of Learning and Changing* (excerpted from pp. 9, 12, 199, 200), ©1994 by Addison-Wesley Publishing Company, Inc. Reprinted by permission of the publisher.

Fordyce, J. K., & Weil, R. (1979). *Managing with people: A manager's handbook for organization development methods* (2nd Ed.) (pp. 13-16). Reading, MA: Addison Wesley. Rights returned to authors. Excerpts are reprinted in Appendix A by permission of author's widow, Hilde Fordyce, and coauthor, Raymond Weil.

Harrison, Roger. *The Collected Papers of Roger Harrison*, excerpts as submitted. Copyright 1995 by Roger Harrison. Excerpts are reprinted in Chapter 8 by permission of Jossey-Bass Publishers.

Weihrich, H. (1982). The TOWS Matrix—A Tool for Situational Analysis, *Long Range Planning*, 15(2), 54-66. Published by Pergamon Press Ltd. Great Britain. Figure 4.1 is reprinted with permission of the publisher.

Introduction

For more than four decades, organizations have been increasingly involved in systematic planned change efforts. These efforts have run parallel to changes in world markets, global economies, increasing competition in many industries, computerization of many industrial functions, increasing discontent with working conditions in some industries, and increasing job insecurity as many organizations downsize, merge, or just cease to be. These changes create considerable pressures for institutions and organizations to engage in self-examination for the purposes of creating more satisfactory work environments and moving beyond a survival mode to a growth-oriented philosophy. The 40-odd years have also produced a growing number of consultants who have developed methodologies from the behavioral sciences to address these organizational needs. Collectively, these programs of change have come to be known under such titles as *organizational development (OD), organization renewal, organization improvement,* or, more recently, *organization transformation.* These titles, in addition, provide an umbrella for a multitude of change technologies involving the total organization or its subsystems, management philosophy and its consequent behaviors, the extent of employee involvement in decisions, and how these factors interface in accomplishing the organization's mission.

As this relatively recent field of applied behavioral science management has developed and expanded, new concepts have emerged, and old concepts have taken on a different look. A language, with its attendant technical jargon, has thereby developed that has tended both to obscure or change the meaning of familiar definitions and, at the same time, to increase the size of our current vocabulary. A considerable amount of misinformation and confusion still exists in the area, even though an information explosion has occurred over the past 40 years through a proliferation of books, journals, articles, courses, seminars, workshops, and organizational consultants and agencies.

The present work of collecting questions from managers started a few years ago during an NTL consultation program with U.S. Army chaplains stationed at 16 bases throughout the United States. Sixteen consultants were asked to list questions concerning OD that were frequently asked of them by army chaplains. These questions were then organized into coherent areas and returned to the consultants to provide answers. Nine consultants returned their responses, which were then collated and distributed in manuscript form to all chaplains and their central office superiors. Later, we discovered that these questions were also typical of those asked by nonmilitary managers.

For the past 3 years, we have been assembling, through several mailed surveys, a number of questions reported by OD consultants that nonmilitary managers frequently asked about OD. These consultants were currently engaged with a variety of organizations and their management. We collated the information they sent us and included our own experience. This process greatly expanded our original set of questions, a sample of which appear in Hanson and Lubin (1989) and now in this book. We recognize that the answers we have presented are tentative and are themselves in the process of change. Our colleagues also made many suggestions and presented us with a couple of dilemmas. One was that some of the questions from the less knowledgeable managers appeared to indicate inexperience as managers. The other problem, related to the first, concerned the inclusion or exclusion of some basic concepts. Some consultants wanted to drop some of the questions; others felt they were necessary for a better understanding of OD and its supportive concepts. We have decided to keep these basic and "dated" questions so as not to ignore some of the managers' requests and to take into account the growing ranks of managers who have not been previously exposed to behavioral science management and OD concepts.

Unfortunately, prior to their entry into the management level, many managers received little or no training in concepts related to behavioral science and human relations. They moved from technically oriented job activities to people-oriented responsibilities that required new and different conceptual frameworks and behaviors. We chose not to ignore their needs. This book is primarily for managers and other students interested in OD who would like an overview of the field without having to commit themselves to a lengthy and in-depth reading on the topic. It is not geared to the level of trained OD consultants or other "experts" in the field. The question-and-answer format is easy to read and reflects those areas about which managers currently want information. The questions are divided into topic areas to facilitate easy identification of those areas with which the reader is most concerned. The reader may discover some redundancy or repetition in the responses. This is due primarily to the relatedness of some of the questions and the similarity of the concepts, processes, and procedures discussed. Rather than referring the reader to another section, we chose to give a complete response so that the reader would not have to flip pages back and forth to get all the relevant information concerning the question. For example, the steps in developing an OD program are very similar to the steps in developing a team-building program, though on a smaller scale; and the material on "concern for science" in Chapter 3 and Appendix B on "laboratory approach" contain an identical passage, on the moral obligations of the scientist, that is appropriate to both sections.

Our rationale for the sequence of topics is, first, to introduce the reader to some basic concepts that underlie OD. We chose basic concepts to precede "What Is OD?" because many of these terms are used in defining OD. For the new manager or student, these descriptions will provide some familiarity with a new language; for more sophisticated readers, it will provide a review of concepts. We then move from some general statements and values to more specific questions concerning the organization and the manager. With this basic orientation, questions then deal with the OD consultant and the consultation process. The section on OD evaluation and diagnosis switches to a more "how-to" description to give practical information on "getting started." Once readers have satisfied their initial curiosity, their appetites may be whetted sufficiently to motivate them to read further. They are referred to the reference list at the end of the book, which contains many readings that survey the field in more detail. We hope that managers, consultants, teachers, and other change agents will find the book useful as educational support for the clients and students with whom they are involved.

What Are Some Basic Concepts Used in Organization Development (OD)?

What is experiential learning?

Several elements in the experiential learning approach have more potency than a purely cognitive, classroom approach for implementing the goals of a training program. Whereas more traditional methods of education, such as lectures, panel discussions, and seminars, assume a passive recipient, the learnings from experiential training emerge from the participants' actual experiences and are processed and conceptualized both by participants and consultant-trainers.

Creating more effective leaders, problem solvers, communicators, and decision makers involves the learning of skills that are analogous, in some ways, to driving an automobile or playing football. In developing these more physical types of skills, one usually finds that reading or lectures may contribute to the understanding of the skill but are relatively ineffective in developing the skill itself. A variety of physical and emotional factors make up the learning process in addition to the purely intellectual ones. The best way to learn a skill is to experience it and practice it: For example, one may read about the rules of the road, but one learns to drive an automobile by getting behind the steering wheel and operating the vehicle.

Experiential learning frequently is used in conjunction with lectures and reading assignments. For example, rather than just reading or hearing about decision making and/or group action, participants in a training program may be given a problem on which they must reach some agreement as a group. During the resulting discussion, many types of decisions are made, and these have different types of effects on group members' interactions and involvement. At the end of the activity, the group members process their interactions to learn how decisions were made and how these decisions affected group members' commitments to the final product. At this point, cognitive material (theory) may be introduced, which is better understood because of the experience that the members have just been through.

Another element present in experiential learning but not considered in the lecture method is the affective component of learning. Feelings and the attitudes and perceptions that they support strongly influence the learning process and determine, to a large extent, how we will use what we learn. For example, events associated with strong positive or negative feelings are remembered for much longer periods of time than events associated with neutral or no feelings. Another example can be taken from our own experience in working with the police and the members of a community (Bell, Cleveland, Hanson, & O'Connell, 1969). Attitudes and prejudices on both sides colored the perceptions that each group had of the other, thereby creating negative stereotypes. Only through face-to-face confrontation, during which both groups were able to test their assumptions about each other, look at the behaviors that supported the stereotypes they had of each other, examine some of the feelings or emotions that supported these stereotypes, and work together in a problem-solving manner, were the two groups able to understand the sources of their conflict. The experiential approach is able to reach the affective resources in individuals and make them available for both personal and professional growth.

What is the laboratory approach?

The emphasis placed on problem solving and scientific inquiry in the workshop setting deserves special attention. The laboratory learning approach places high value on fully utilizing the concepts and methods of the social and behavioral sciences, particularly as they apply to the practical affairs of everyday living. Central to the scientific method are such values as objectivity, integrity, and the pursuit of information relevant to the issues, regardless of vested interest and political expediency. As a result, decision making and problem solving can be accomplished on the basis of objective evidence. Even the term *laboratory* carries scientific implications and suggests experimental inquiry and scientific methodology (Benne,

Bradford, & Lippitt, 1964, p. 3). Participants directly or indirectly perceive that they all are scientists in that they observe behavior, collect data, and develop assumptions and hypotheses about people and life. Because they are untrained scientists, however, their biases and prejudices distort their picture of reality, and they continuously fall short of testing their assumptions. In the training environment, participants are encouraged to test their assumptions about other group members rather than merely to assume that these are true.

Because scientists have the moral obligation to consider all the facts in any problem situation, the person who is trying to make life a science must remember that other people's feelings are facts. In the human relations laboratory, the attitudes and feelings of others must be taken into consideration and weighed with as much respect as one accords to any other data. The human facts revealed then become available for improved theory construction and more realistic choices.

Some participants arrive at a training event with narrow or unsatisfying ways of experiencing life and handling life's dilemmas. Although their typical (fight-flight) responses have frequently not been very effective, they continue to use them. One of the goals of human relations laboratory training is to break up this pattern and to create space for people to experience and do things differently. The idea of the participant's involvement in scientific inquiry and experimentation helps to promote an atmosphere of flexibility.

What is human relations training?

The term *human relations training* has generally been replaced by the term *human interaction laboratory.* Individuals who join a training group have personal goals that they hope to achieve through group interactions and are willing to pay for this opportunity. The goals of training groups may overlap the goals of therapy groups in that they both provide an opportunity for individual group members to learn more about themselves, their impact on other individuals in the group setting, some of the dynamics that occur in small groups, and how they themselves affect these processes (Hanson, Rothaus, Johnson, & Lyle, 1966; Hanson, Rothaus, O'Connell, & Wiggins, 1969, 1970). Training groups, however, usually attract or solicit individuals who already are effective in their personal and vocational lives but who may want to increase their effectiveness. A further goal of the training group, therefore, is to create an environment in which this type of learning can take place.

Because the training group is the arena in which the processes that go on in other groups can be studied as they occur in the here-and-now interactions of the group members, another goal of human relations training is to assist individuals to become more effective participants in their back-home groups. For this reason, the training group, as opposed to other groups, pays close attention to its ongoing processes. Here-and-now behavior is examined as it occurs within the individual (feelings, perceptions), between individuals (communication, styles of influence), and among group members (decision making, group norms).

Members are encouraged to express curiosity about personal, interpersonal, and group events. As scientists, individuals will collect data (feelings, attitudes, perceptions), build hypotheses, and test them out with other group members. Thus, through inquiry and sharing, group members can abstract relevant learnings from their experiences.

The focus of attention in the human relations training group is on the development of the group from relative chaos into an effective learning unit. This includes the development of relationships within the group and the identification of personal styles and resources of members. Group members have the right to withhold any personal information not relevant to the goals of the group, and in-depth analysis of individual personalities or back-home problems is discouraged. However, back-home, work-related problems may be discussed when they are relevant to the task or ongoing activity or when meaningful relationships are perceived between what is happening in the group and some back-home event.

Management of information and decision making are achieved primarily through group interaction and group consensus. The goal of group leaders is to facilitate these processes rather than to control them. The expression and sharing of feelings, ideas, and beliefs that are relevant to individual and group goals are reinforced by group leaders and most members. Again, the exception is when individual members are threatened by the expression of feelings and attempt to block this type of material.

To aid in the setting of group standards, training group leaders frequently act as models to facilitate behaviors that move the group in the direction of openness, exchange of feedback, and risk taking. Other group standards and norms emerge as the result of interactions within the group and the group's assessment of behaviors that facilitate or hinder individual and group progress. Task-oriented behaviors do not receive as much support as do socioemotional behaviors. As a consequence, group members need to create a balance in which the behavior of task-oriented individuals is seen as legitimate and valued when the demands of the situation require it. The development of group standards and norms to facilitate goal achievement requires continuous monitoring and processing.

The development of a climate of trust, acceptance, and mutual support is extremely important in enabling individuals to share their here-and-now experiences. The group's movement toward its goals is not a straight-line progression but oscillates over the period of the group's life. Goals may need to be redefined or clarified periodically, but as long as the group members feel that there is some movement, they generally remain committed to the goals.

What is a T-group?

A T-group is the special vehicle through which most of the learning takes place in a human relations training laboratory or, as it is currently called, a human interaction laboratory. Much of the information regarding human relations training applies here. There may be several T-groups in one laboratory workshop. A typical T-group (training group, originally called a basic skills training group; Bradford, Gibb, & Benne, 1964) consists of 10 to 12 members who meet with a trainer and perhaps a co-trainer and work together as a group for the duration of the training event. The group has no formal agenda, no guidelines concerning appropriate or inappropriate behavior, and no clear-cut leadership. The function of the trainer is to facilitate the efforts of the participants to learn about their own behavior and how that behavior affects the development of the group. Participants also learn about aspects of group behavior such as communication processes, decision making, norm setting, and conflict management.

The trainer does not lead the group or create dependence by directing and controlling group activities. The trainer does provide a model for group members by demonstrating openness, listening skills, and the non-defensive acceptance of feedback. The trainer displays a willingness to accept responsibility for, or "own," his or her own feelings and behaviors and to share personal feelings and reactions with other members of the group. Openness on the part of trainers is an important factor in encouraging risk taking on the part of the participants. The subsequent openness among group members provides the data around which a learning process can be built. Because the trainers do not provide the type of leadership that participants expect, a leadership vacuum is created, and the group members attempt to fill it in order to get the group moving in one direction or another. Their attempts to fill this vacuum become further data for the group to work with. In short, the group's learning experience includes observation and examination of individual members' behavior, how this behavior influences other members, how members' interactions affect and are affected by the process within the group, and how group members resolve the issue of authority as they attempt to deal with the somewhat ambiguous role of the trainer. Toward the later phases of the group's life, the members begin to assess what they have learned about themselves and other group members through a mutual exchange of feedback.

As group members gain more confidence in handling issues within the group, the role of the trainers becomes less controversial, and the trainers are more free to contribute to the group as persons who have some special resources rather than as leaders. However, although the trainers become more like peers in relation to the other participants as the group develops, they rarely are considered as just another group member. By virtue of their assigned roles, they are associated with whatever stereotypes the members may have of the role of "leader." The effective trainer will use this phenomenon to help participants explore the extent to which their perceptions and reactions are influenced by such stereotypes.

In summary, the T-group represents an arena in which many of the personal, interpersonal, and group events that occur in back-home groups (but are usually not acknowledged or handled) can be confronted and worked through in an atmosphere that enables the participants to learn from these experiences. T-groups have been tried in organizations as an OD intervention with limited success. The focus of group dynamics and group leadership that is a major part of team building has been borrowed from T-group methodology.

What is group process?

To illustrate what *process* means, let us use a training group, or T-group, as an example, noting that these process issues are common to all groups (e.g., work teams, staff meetings, management conferences, social groups).

The term *process* refers to how people work together, as contrasted to what (content, task, or problem) they are working on. The term is interchangeable with *group dynamics*, that is, how decisions are made, how conflict is handled, how people communicate with each other, and how groups interface on common issues or problems. For example, if a group or team member feels angry, that anger is content; how that member expresses (or does not express) the feeling is process. Content issues can be topics that arise outside the group's or work team's life, such as members' family or job situations or the effect of the current political system on the economy. Such content issues are referred to as *there-and-then* topics. Other content issues can concern events that are caused by the group and directly related to its own activity. These content issues can center on relationships among group members, a task that the group is working on, a decision that the group needs to make, or the development of personal or group goals. While the group is dealing with this content, different members of the group may respond in different ways: Feelings of anger may be generated, some members may withdraw, others may attack, and still others may confront the issue more creatively. A few members may increase their levels of participation, become more "alive," and feel more involved and influential. Pairing or subgrouping may occur, which leads to intragroup conflict, creating an atmosphere of tension. When these events are discussed as they occur, the group is focusing on process rather than on task. Process events are always here and now—what is happening in this group now. They often go unnoticed until someone identifies them and the group is then motivated to explore what happened.

When the discussion takes place after the process event, the process becomes the content. At these times, the distinction between process and content becomes fuzzy. For example, in talking about how outside norms are affecting behavior in the group, the discussion of process becomes the content. During a discussion of a process (the topic), a process event (here and now) can occur (e.g., when one group member becomes angry with another member who makes an irrelevant intervention). The group members then must decide whether to proceed with the discussion of a process (the content) or stop and focus on the angry interchanges between the two members (process). The following examples of content and process statements may help to clarify the distinction.

Member: "My husband says I'm insecure." (content)
Trainer: "How do you feel about that?" (process)
Member: "I could never get a straight answer from my boss." (content)
Trainer: "How would you like me to respond to you?" (process)
Member: "I'm always called on to do favors or to give advice. I always seem to be giving and not getting." (content)
Trainer: "Have the same demands been made on you here in the group?" (process)
Member: "Everyone seems so polite here. No one says anything negative, including me." (process)

Member: "It seems as though we never complete a discussion before we jump to another topic." (process)

Member: "At our group session yesterday, I found myself becoming extremely angry at Joan. I know she was withholding her feelings from me, but what puzzled me most was the degree of anger I felt!" (a discussion of a process event becomes a content discussion)

Trainer: "How do you feel toward Joan now?" (back to process)

One of the major functions of the trainer or team leader is to facilitate members' awareness of the group's processes and to aid the members in learning to identify them. Focusing on the dynamics of what is going on in the here and now affords group members the opportunity to look at their behavior in a social setting and to assess to what extent they contribute or do not contribute to that setting. Sensitivity to group process provides group members with a social reality that quite often is missed or avoided in everyday living and in back-home groups.

To help a group or team become more process oriented, the trainer or leader may want to direct the group's attention to the similarities or differences between the group (team) as a social system and the culture (organization) at large. In this way, the transfer of learning between the two systems can be facilitated.

The training group is a miniature social system in which the members must surface one process issue after another. Thus, process issues concerning goal setting, decision making, norm setting, task and maintenance functions, group atmosphere, and conflict management are dealt with as they emerge in the group. It is this attention to process that provides the group with some of its most stimulating experiences and is one of the most powerful forces that facilitates group involvement and commitment.

What are some of the processes at the organizational level?

Much of what has been covered in "group process" applies at the organizational level. If we consider that all organizations are made up of teams (groups), team building and working with teams can be an important part of an OD program. How the team defines its role in the achievement of the organization's mission is related to how it collects information, clarifies its goals, makes decisions, and solves problems. A major function of the team leader or manager is to provide the organizational perspective within which the team does its work.

A significant process involves the organization's culture—that is, assumptions, beliefs, values, and attitudes that govern the behavior of its members and their feelings about the organization. An overriding philosophy that provides a framework for policies regarding employees and customers and the way this philosophy is implemented are also part of the process to be addressed. Vaill (1989b) saw OD as "a process for observing process" and stated that "sadly, the field has drifted away from its goal of serving as a process for improving process" (p. 262).

In an organization, no team or group works in complete isolation. Teams, or groups, if they have a history, can form their own culture. If groups get into conflict with each other, their individual identities may be threatened, thereby sustaining the conflict and maintaining the intragroup culture (Schein, 1985). In any organization these groups or teams interface, increasing the possibility of intergroup conflict. Some of these groupings are management/labor, night shift/day shift, management technicians/scientists, and home office/field office. On an informal basis, groups may form along racial, ethnic, and gender lines. The organization also interfaces with its external environment and other organizations. For a more elaborate examination of intergroup conflict, see Chapter 8 on interdepartmental relations.

What is meant by *here and now* versus *there and then?*

One of the primary characteristics of learning groups, team building, and OD methodology is the focus on what is occurring here and now, among the group and departmental members and within individual members themselves. This focus is difficult to maintain because people are in the habit of continually dealing with things that happened yesterday, last month, or last year, planning for things that will happen in the coming minutes, hours, days, or years, and looking at what is happening elsewhere in the world. These times and places are *there and then,* that is, events occurring outside of the group at a different time. In addition, people spend much of their time wishing that things were better or different, desiring this thing or that experience. There seems to be little time in the real world to stop the action (particularly in an ongoing interpersonal transaction) and reflect on what is occurring to and within the self at this moment and at this place. For example, if a member of a team is experiencing a feeling that is related to an outside event, his or her experience of that event is here and now, although the event itself may be there and then. Most of us, however, would focus on the content of the event as it occurred in the past. It is important in this case for the participant to focus on how he or she is experiencing the event now rather than to go into a detailed description of the event itself. The story of an event usually does not include a description of how the person feels now, as he or she relives the event itself. The event is "dead" and cannot be changed. Although we may not be able to change the world, we can change our experience of the world. It is a different matter when a participant has a sudden insight about an ongoing experience in the group and can relate or apply that insight to an event or situation outside the group. It is perfectly legitimate at that time for the participant to make the linkage and to describe the nature of the insight and its relationship to the outside work situation—to find an application or use for a learning that occurred in the here and now.

In the here and now, members are forced to assume responsibility for what they are doing and saying now, rather than focusing on issues in the past or future to explain or to justify their current actions and attitudes. By failing to develop this habit or skill, people fail to realize, or to be aware of, much of what they are feeling or experiencing at the moment and how this experience affects the process of making choices. That is, the more aware we are of all of our experiences (feelings, perceptions, body sensations, expectations, attitudes, etc.), the more data are available to us for making decisions or taking action.

Most people have difficulty working through here-and-now interactions, particularly when they are negative or stressful. It is much easier to describe a stressful interaction that occurred yesterday than it is to deal with it competently as it is occurring. An effective learning group or team is a relatively safe place in which members can learn to handle here-and-now interactions in more effective ways. Because the here-and-now focus is the most risk-taking situation, and thus the most threatening part of the group's activities, participants will avoid it whenever possible until a climate of trust and acceptance is developed in the group and they feel able to take such risks. At the same time, this focus provides the most exciting, most energy-inducing, and ultimately most satisfying experiences of group or team life.

We frequently hear terms like *task* and *maintenance* behaviors. What is the difference?

Early studies on group behavior identified roles that individuals assumed within the group (or team) context. A number of years ago, Benne and Sheats (1948) identified three classes of member roles—group task roles, group-building and maintenance roles, and individual roles—and listed a number of functions within each role. Bales (1958) later identified first two and then three emerging roles: task (idea man), social-emotional (best liked), and deviant (not well liked). Bass (1962, 1967) identified similar group roles, which he called *self-orientation, interaction-orientation,* and *task-orientation.* These three studies appear to have identified group roles that are consistent with each other.

Task functions are concerned with getting the job done, or accomplishing the task the team has before it. Organizational objectives take precedence over individual needs. *Maintenance* functions are important to the morale of the work group. They maintain good harmonious working relationships among the members and create an atmosphere that enables each member to contribute maximally. Individual needs are addressed significantly more than organizational objectives by maintenance-oriented members. *Individual* role behaviors are focused on getting personal needs met in the group. Individuals may come into a work setting or group with a set of personal needs and an expectation that these needs will be met. Unfortunately, the expression of these needs, if ignored, may be acted out in ways disruptive to the work of the group. Individual or personal needs are dealt with more effectively in therapeutic groups. Table 1.1 illustrates some of the behaviors reflecting each role behavior.

For a team to work effectively, all these functions (task, maintenance, individual) are necessary. To focus only on task may be to sacrifice individuals' feelings and their needs to be acknowledged and supported. To focus only on maintenance may be to ignore or devalue task behaviors and become preoccupied with process. In this case, very little work may be accomplished. There needs to be a happy balance between task and maintenance behaviors. Individual role behaviors may create an atmosphere of tension and conflict. These behaviors can also energize a group and act as a catalyst for other members to examine their own effectiveness in handling situations in which their own expectations as to how people should behave are violated.

Table 1.1   Group Role Behaviors

Task	Maintenance	Individual
Stating or clarifying task or problem	Facilitating participation of others (gatekeeping)	Criticizing Obstructing
Establishing procedures	Checking for understanding	Dominating
Asking for and giving information	Giving support and encouragement to others	Seeking attention
Summarizing	Helping others to test their assumptions	Playing the victim role
Keeping group on topic	Checking for feelings	
Integrating	Mediating	Not taking things seriously
Evaluating	Actively participating and observing	Crusading for some personal cause

SOURCE: Hanson, 1981.

As work groups or teams mature, there is a more appropriate balance of task and maintenance behaviors, and dysfunctional, self-oriented behaviors tend to drop out.

What are norms?

Norms are standards or ground rules that influence or control organizational, group, or team behavior. They are beliefs or desires held or accepted by the majority of people in the organization about what behaviors should or should not take place in the organization or in a work team or group. They can emerge from within the group or infiltrate the group from without (i.e., the organizational culture in which the group is embedded, or the culture at large). Indeed, norms are one of the most important and often one of the most elusive aspects of organizational culture (discussed later in this chapter). For purposes of this chapter, however, we will discuss norms as they relate to the work team or group, recognizing that the statements are also applicable to the organization as a whole.

Many norms are formal in the sense they are written out as rules, regulations, procedures, or policies. Whether a written policy becomes a norm, however, depends upon the extent to which it governs behavior: That is, do people actually behave in a way consistent with the norm? If their behavior differs from the written norm, then the behavior is the norm, not the written statement. For example, the official written statement may say, "Staff meetings will begin at 9:00 a.m. every Wednesday morning." Team members usually drift in between 9:15 and 9:30, so the meeting typically gets started at 9:30 a.m. Coming late and starting at 9:30 is the norm, not the written statement. If the meeting typically starts at 9:00 a.m., then the written statement is the norm. A norm is not a norm unless people behave in keeping with it.

Some norms may be explicit, as when everyone, or almost everyone, is aware of them. They may be statements of how the group or team wants to operate, agreed upon by group members. Again, if the explicitly stated norm is not followed by team members, then it is not a norm. Many norms are implicit in that very few people or no one is aware of them, but they govern group behavior nevertheless. The implicit norms are frequently those that are adhered to in contrast to the formal or explicitly stated norms. For example, at every staff meeting, team members may sit in the same seat, although no seats have been specifically assigned to members. One day John sits in the chair that James has been occupying at staff meetings. John is immediately challenged by James as having taken his seat. John responds that seats have not been assigned and he can sit where he pleases. James is upset and insists on having *his* seat. A norm has been violated, and the team may now have to examine whether it is a useful norm. The implicit norm in the previous example of the 9:00 a.m. staff meetings is the late arrival of team members.

Implicit norms frequently are not discovered until someone breaks one; when it becomes obvious to someone that the team avoids certain topics, interactions, or behaviors; or when certain behaviors, or operations are engaged in that have no real utility for the team, but persist anyway until someone challenges them. Statements such as "We've always done it this way," "Bill is out of uniform, no tie," "Never volunteer," "Cover your ass (CYA)," "Let's stick to the facts and keep feelings out of this!" "Don't rock the boat," and "As long as you don't bring it up, it won't be clear whether we are violating a policy" indicate that implicit norms are operating to which the majority of the members subscribe, even though they are not discussed or explicitly agreed upon.

Some norms exist that are not known to any group or team members or are, at best, vaguely sensed by some. These norms have to do with values, beliefs, and behaviors so ingrained and accepted that they rarely are surfaced for examination. For example, as angry as team members may get toward each other, the question of whether to kill each other would never come up as an option for the resolution of the conflict. Included in the areas of unconscious norms are strong taboos involving sex, religion, family, and loyalties to institutions.

Norms can facilitate or hinder team progress or functioning. An implicit norm that says, "The expression and discussion of feelings is not a legitimate area of concern to this team" will hinder team functioning, particularly when the issues with which the team is dealing evoke strong emotions. The opposite type of norm, of course, will facilitate team functioning.

Norms can be explicit and facilitate team functioning, or they can be explicit and hinder the team. They can be implicit and still facilitate team movement, or they can be implicit and hinder team effectiveness. For example, a team may have an explicit and facilitative norm that says, "We want to learn more about how we are functioning in this team and exchange feedback," but also, simultaneously, an implicit and hindering norm that says, "You have to be careful here or you can really get hurt—play it safe!" As a consequence, team behavior may be excessively polite and superficial (the implicit norm dominating).

Conflicts may occur when the values, goals, and beliefs of individual team members (individual norms) run counter to the team norms. When this happens, several things may occur: The individual may exert influence to change the team norm, conform to the norm, continue in the team as a "deviant," or decide to leave the team.

One may ask, "Why do norms exist?" Generally, norms serve several purposes. One is goal achievement. In order for a group or team to achieve a goal, team members have to govern and maintain those behaviors that are perceived as facilitating this purpose. Members who do not adhere to these norms will be seen as a threat to the team's accomplishing its goal. Second, norms are supported that help the group or team maintain itself. Intact groups or teams do not easily tolerate behaviors that they perceive as having potential to destroy group integrity. Third, in order to maintain itself and to prosper, a group or team develops norms that increase its attractiveness to team members. Members are encouraged (often pressured) to report personal achievements or to work toward achieving honors or prestige that might reflect positively on the group as a whole. Last, norms provide a social or consensual reality against which the individual may assess his or her own reality (e.g., how much he or she is in touch with, or in tune with, the perceptions, judgments, beliefs, attitudes, values, etc., of other group members or members of his or her own social group).

The presence of norms is an inevitable characteristic common to all groups, work teams, and organizations. One of the primary tasks for group leaders, managers, and group members is to help their team or group identify the particular norms under which they are operating and to assess their effect on team or group functioning.

What is organizational culture?

Organizational culture describes the patterns for how to do things that result in some order or regularity in the way the organization functions. These elements include attitudes, assumptions, beliefs, implicit ground rules or norms, and conventions. They also include how rules, regulations, and policies are formulated and implemented. The culture sets standards for how people relate to each other, what behaviors are appropriate or inappropriate, and what issues or problems are legitimate or not legitimate for discussion, exploration, and examination. These standards represent norms, which are one major aspect of organizational culture and often exert powerful influences on organizational behavior—even when they are not explicitly stated or visible to most people within the organization. Burke (1994) believed that the primary element in a given culture "is a unique pattern of norms, standards or rules of conduct to which members conform. Other significant elements . . . are its authority structure and ways of exercising power, values, rewards and ways of dispensing them and communication patterns" (p. 9). Schein (1985) saw organizational culture as a set of basic assumptions and beliefs that reflect how the organization views itself and its environment. The assumptions and beliefs are held by the members of the organization and function below the level of awareness. They are never examined because the members have learned that these assumptions and beliefs have been successful in solving organizational problems of "internal integration" over a long period of time. What we see on the surface are "artifacts" and "values" that arise from this deeper level of assumptions but "are not the essence of the culture" (pp. 6-7).

To set up any type of change program, whether training or organization development, it is critical to understand the culture of the work setting. To ignore the organizational culture is to create considerable difficulties for oneself and even make it impossible to institute any change program. For example, within the organizational culture, a norm may be operating that says that the study of interpersonal relationships and effective leadership styles is not a legitimate area of concern in this organization. The only legitimate areas open for examination are those involving getting the job done and increasing production. If this norm is operating, any program that deals with interpersonal relations and leadership styles will be met with strong resistance and may even fail. However, a program that addresses itself to job or production issues, if successful, may serve as a vehicle for dealing with broader interpersonal issues later and may eventually effect changes in organizational norms.

Many parts of the organizational culture are highly visible, such as organizational structure, job titles and descriptions, formal authority networks, operating policies and practices, and the ways in which productivity is rewarded. On the other hand, many components of the organizational culture are far less visible but nonetheless powerful in affecting employee behavior. These include patterns of power and influence; norms and loyalties of work groups; perceptions of who you can trust and how much risk you can take; personal values that affect people's perceptions of work roles; feelings and needs of employees; how people relate to each other, to their own group, and to other departments; and ways in which human talents are identified and rewarded. This informal (sub rosa) organization contains many of the not-so-visible parts of the culture and is often used to "get around" (even sabotage) the rules, regulations, and policies of the formal, highly visible organization.

Control of the rate of production by members of the work unit is an example of an implicit norm. The organization sets the rate of production at 10 units per work shift in order to receive bonus compensation. The norm that group members subscribe to is between 8 to 12 units per work shift, even though 15 to 18 units are not too difficult to achieve. If any member starts producing above the norm, group pressure is exerted to bring the deviant back into line. The concern of the work unit members, of course, is that the bonus rate will be reset at a higher level per work shift.

One major goal of organization development in many change programs that attempt to increase effectiveness of an organization is to diagnose the organization's culture and replace outmoded, ineffective ways of doing things and relating to others with more productive and growth-producing norms.

What is participative management (PM)?

The onset of the Industrial Revolution created a work environment in which work was fractionated into minute sets of repetitive activities, workers were powerless to influence or control their working conditions, and workers were socially isolated, thereby becoming alienated. As a consequence of these factors, work became meaningless. It has also been found that feelings of powerlessness, meaninglessness, and social isolation can lead to physical and emotional ill health. A series of studies conducted over a period of 50 years, beginning with the Hawthorne project in the 1920s and 1930s, indicated that job satisfaction and productivity were related to worker participation in goal setting, decision making, problem solving, and change. These activities appeared to satisfy basic human needs for control of one's life (work life), for meaningful work, and for social interactions with other workers. Participative management (PM) can range from putting suggestions in the employee suggestion box to being on the board of directors. For the most part, however, PM is an effort to give employees an opportunity to contribute to group goals, to participate in decisions that affect their work, and to be involved in problem solving and change efforts. The overall goal is to increase employees' interest in and commitment to the organization by giving them a feeling of ownership in the system in which they work. Goal setting, decision making, and problem solving done in a group or team setting rather than by individual managers, written reports, or chain of command offers several advantages. A group or team context can develop more good ideas, produce mutual interdependence and feedback, and coordinate efforts more effectively. The group or team also provides opportunity for face-to-face group discussions that develop social support for decisions, solutions, and changes, and fulfill needs for social interaction (Sashkin, 1984). These goals are consistent with OD values. Sometimes failures of PM have been due to a lack of involvement of managers or a confusion of PM with a laissez-faire management style.

We have heard of Theory X and Theory Y. Now there is a Theory Z. What are the differences?

Theories X and Y, as outlined by McGregor (1960), are two styles of management based on differing assumptions about work and human nature. The basic questions addressed in this classic study were, What type of organizational climate is conducive to human growth, and what are the assumptions of top management (both implicit and explicit) about the most effective way to manage people? The whole character of the enterprise is determined by these assumptions.

Theory X stems from traditional management philosophy and arose from the practices of managers during the Industrial Revolution. It is militaristic in style and based on "carrot-and-stick" incentives that motivate workers by reward and punishment. Its assumptions, as described by McGregor (1960), are as follows:

1. "The average human being has an inherent dislike of work and will avoid it if he can." (p. 33)
2. "Because of this human characteristic of dislike of work, most people must be coerced, controlled, directed, or threatened with punishment to get them to put forth adequate effort toward the achievement of organizational objectives." (p. 34)
3. "The average human being prefers to be directed, wishes to avoid responsibility, has relatively little ambition, wants security above all." (p. 34)

Since the 1920s, management has moved more in the direction of humanitarian considerations, such as more equitable and generous treatment of employees, reduced economic hardships, and safe and pleasant work environments. As of the 1950s and 1960s, however, management has made these improvements without changing its basic philosophy of management. During this time, increasing information about human behavior has led to the beginnings of a newer theory of motivation and of managing people—Theory Y. The assumptions underlying Theory Y, as described by McGregor (1960), are as follows:

1. "The expenditure of physical and mental effort in work is as natural as play or work." (p. 47)
2. "External control and threat of punishment are not the only means for bringing about effort toward organizational objectives. Man will exercise self direction and self control in the service of objectives to which he is committed." (p. 47)
3. "Commitment to objectives is a function of the rewards associated with their achievement" (i.e., "satisfaction of ego and self actualization needs"). (p. 47)
4. "The average human being learns, under proper conditions, not only to accept but to seek responsibility." (p. 48)
5. "The capacity to exercise a relatively high degree of imagination, ingenuity and creativity in the solution of organizational problems is widely, not narrowly, distributed in the population." (p. 48)
6. "Under conditions of modern industrial life, the intellectual potentialities of the average human being are only partially utilized." (p. 48)

Theory X depends upon the exercise of authority through direction and control. Theory Y, on the other hand, attempts to create conditions whereby individuals can achieve their own goals through achieving organizational objectives. Obviously, organizations today are not clearly one or the other, but contain elements of both theories. In Hall (1988), a picture of the average individual in our culture is drawn from a composite of over 1,000 studies of human behavior. From this profile, he concluded that more than two thirds of people by nature reflect the Theory Y assumptions: That is, they are bright, flexible, self-directed, social, ambitious, and committed to peers and organizations. "Only about ten percent are indeed lazy, ineffective individuals described in a theory X view" (pp. 54, 55). In effect, if managers use Theory Y practices, they will be on target with 7 out of 10 individuals, whereas with Theory X they will miss 90% of the time.

Theory Z (Ouchi, 1981; Ouchi & Jaeger, 1978) appears to be an extension of Theory Y in that it espouses consensual decision making, individual responsibility, informal control, and a holistic concern for the employee. Employees are "guaranteed" long-term employment with relatively slow movement up the career ladder. This philosophy reflects a type of participative management in which participative teams are developed with defined roles. The stress is on interdependence. Theory Z organizations are more typical of Japanese society, in which harmony and subordination of the individual to the group are highly valued. In many companies, employees appear to be taken into the organization as family members. In the United States, higher value is placed upon individualism and pragmatism. Schein (1985) acknowledged the value of lifetime employment and managements' concern about their employees, but stated he did not know their underlying lifetime assumptions concerning policy, values, and practices upon which the organization is built. Does the company own the individual? If individuals leave an organization, are they labeled as disloyal? Will this label follow the individuals as they seek employment elsewhere? With the influx of Japanese plants opening in the United States, modified forms of Theory Z are being tested on the American employee.

What is a team?

Much of what is presented here and later in this chapter is expanded from an article by Hanson and Lubin (1988). Every organization consists of work teams, or at least a single work team. No one person in an organization works completely independently of everyone else. Everyone is related in some way to somebody; otherwise, it is not really an organization. A one-person business is not an organization. Teams consist of people who have some relatedness to each other or reason for working together as a function of doing their jobs or accomplishing a task. A team may be relatively permanent, such as a supervisor and his subordinates, a manager and her supervisors, and a president and his vice presidents or top-level managers. A manager may also be the head of several teams. People, moreover, may belong to more than one team (e.g., a manager may be part of a management team and also have his or her own team of subordinates). Teams may be temporary and have a life together only as long as it takes to accomplish a particular task (e.g., task forces, ad hoc committees). A team may also be dispersed throughout a large geographical area, as is true of large organizations with offices and plants at different locations. Part of the task of an OD program is to identify the teams and who works on which team. Figure 1.1 is an oversimplified and incomplete organizational chart of a general psychiatric hospital that illustrates the complexity of teams and their interdependence. Not included are the many staff and consultation services (medical, surgical, laboratories, etc.).

The development of a well-functioning team takes a considerable amount of time and effort to accomplish. It is difficult even for people who are well grounded in human interaction learning and group process to create and maintain a well-functioning team. It is extremely important for team members to recognize and accept their own needs, to be sensitive to the needs of team members, and to maintain some balance between these needs. A principle of effective team functioning is accomplished when members have both high concern for their own needs and high concern for the needs of others. These needs are also analogous to the major concerns of management, which are high concern for task and high concern for people (morale). Some of the characteristics of an effective team are as follows:

1. A shared sense of purpose or common goals and a willingness of each team member to work toward achieving these goals.

2. An awareness of and interest in its own process and the examination of norms that are operating within the group.

3. Identification of its own resources and the utilization of these resources depending upon the needs of the team at any given time. At these times the group is willing to accept the influence and leadership of the member whose resources are most relevant to the immediate task.

4. A continuing effort on the part of group members to listen and to clarify what is being said, and an interest shown in what others say and feel and in hearing them out.

5. Encouragement and free expression of differences of opinion. The team does not demand narrow conformity or adherence to formats that inhibit freedom of movement and expression.

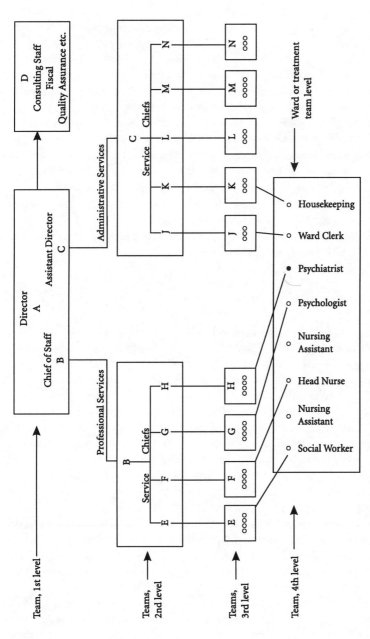

Figure 1.1. Simple Organizational Chart of a General Psychiatric Hospital Depicting Work Teams and Multiple Membership

21

6. Willingness to address conflict and stay with it until it is either resolved or managed in a way that does not reduce the effectiveness of the individuals involved.

7. Energy exerted toward problem solving rather than being drained off by interpersonal issues or competitive struggles.

8. A balance of roles that are shared to facilitate both the accomplishment of task and feelings of group cohesion and morale.

9. View of mistakes as a source for learning rather than an occasion for punishment; encouragement of risk taking and creativity.

10. Responsiveness to the changing needs of team members and to the external environment to which the team is related.

11. Commitment to periodic evaluation of team performance.

12. Attractiveness to members, who identify with the team and see it as a source of both professional and personal growth.

13. Recognition that the development of a climate of trust is the crucial element needed to facilitate all of the above elements.

What are support systems?

Generally speaking, most of us belong to many groups or social systems (e.g., family, work, school, friendships) from which we receive many types of support. These types of support may include providing feedback, giving assistance and resources when needed, being a sounding board as a check against social realities, or providing technical and emotional support and challenge. The standards or norms of the groups influence our perceptions, attitudes, values, beliefs, and personal goals and how we implement them. Much of the power of these groups lies in the fact that they help us to feel good about ourselves, to have a sense of belonging, to feel we are important to others, to challenge us to stretch ourselves and to act as a buffer against the harsh realities of life. Belonging to a support group also means that we are expected to provide support to others (Hanson & Lubin, 1986).

In the work setting it is important to identify individuals and groups from whom one receives and to whom one provides support. It is also important to identify what type of support one gets from different individuals and groups (e.g., technical support from superiors, emotional support from coworkers). An individual from whom one receives support in a particular area (e.g., emotional) may not be in one's department or work team. Some people are more capable of giving support in certain areas than other people. It is important, therefore, to survey the interpersonal environment to assess who can give the particular type of support one needs rather than to expect everything, unrealistically, from one person. A work team can be a support system. Team building may facilitate the supportive elements of many support functions (e.g., feedback, technical appreciation, social interactions, reality testing, belonging, being valued). Many organizations are recognizing the health-inducing function of support systems within their own internal environment. It is an obvious conclusion that employees who feel valued, have a sense of belonging, and receive sustenance from the teams of which they are a part will be more productive in the work setting.

What is synergy?

Synergy or *synergism* is a term frequently used in some of the medical sciences (e.g., pharmacology, physiology). Its dictionary definition (*Webster's New World Dictionary*, 1988) is "1. the simultaneous action of separate agencies which together have greater total effect than the sum of their individual effects; said esp. of drugs. 2. combined or correlated action of different organs or parts of the body; as of muscles working together." Blake and Mouton (1968) used the concept as a basic energy-producing principle in Phases 2 (teamwork, development) and 3 (intergroup development). They defined synergy as "members work[ing] together in a cooperative way so that the total effect is greater than the sum of the separate parts acting independently" (p. 8). One of the purposes of team building is to increase the synergy potential of the group. When team members feel free to express and exchange their thoughts and feelings and to get all this information on the table, the integration and combination of ideas produce data not originally present in the individual members. The synergy principle is one of the advantages of team over individual problem solving. Synergy is evident in team consensus building and almost visibly present in brainstorming sessions. This is an affirmation of the old adage, "Two (or more) heads are better than one." The synergy principle is also potentially present in intergroup or interdepartmental relations. When groups or departments are in competition with each other, they may withhold resources from each other and expend energy and creativity in trying to make the other group lose. This feeds and perpetuates nonproductive interactions and is antithetical to the principle of synergy. When groups or departments cooperate, they pool their resources and channel energy into cooperative efforts. This increases the energy level of both groups and creates conditions for more effective problem solving. "Corporate synergism is achieved when a 'within department' concentration of effort is reenforced by a 'between department' coordination of effort. The total capacity of the corporation to achieve is then more than the sum of efforts of each department considered singly" (Blake & Mouton, 1968, p. 159).

What is team building?

Calling a group or work unit a *team* implies a particular process of working together, in which members identify and fully utilize one another's resources and facilitate their mutual interdependence toward more effective problem solving and task accomplishment. Team building, then, is usually part of an OD effort in which a team studies its own process (how members work together) and takes some action steps to create a climate in which members' energies are directed toward problem solving and maximizing the use of all members' resources in this process.

To help a team study its own workings, managers may sometimes bring in an OD consultant. If managers have these process skills themselves, they may choose to help their own team study its functioning. Consultants or managers may use several approaches, such as helping the team to develop a process orientation and skills in self-observation, data collection, and feedback, and assessing team members' leadership styles and their impact on team functioning. One important aspect of team building is to help a team develop a "model of excellence"[1] against which to measure their own performance. After identifying norms and procedures by which the team functions, consultants or managers may then establish criteria of effectiveness along a number of behavioral and procedural dimensions that provide targets for the team to achieve. For team building to be successful, however, it is important that all team members see the relevance of this self-study to more effective functioning and have a commitment to looking at and critiquing their own behavior.

Team building is indicated when the manager and/or the team are aware of certain symptoms that exist within the team. These symptoms may include such things as low productivity, unresolved conflicts between members that block understanding and tie up team time, members' resources not being utilized appropriately, decisions that are slipping through the cracks or unclear, confusion about who is to do what and when, ineffective staff meetings with little or no participation or problem identification, a general lack of interest and creativity accompanied by apathy and maintaining the status quo, and complaints from users or other departments that the team is not responsive to the needs of others or meeting its responsibilities. Assisting a team to study its own process and to develop more effective ways of operating involves a fair degree of risk. During this activity, conflicts and feelings that may have been kept under wraps for a long time may surface and create considerable tension and anxiety. Members may also fear that their future relationships will be adversely affected by the amount of leveling and exchange of feedback. Although team building may involve considerable risk, the payoff is likely to be much higher in terms of getting things on the table where they can be examined, developing more authentic ways of relating, increasing team members' competence to handle interpersonal conflicts, and creating an atmosphere in which members are not engaged in interpersonal infighting but are using their energies in creative problem solving. As a consequence of the amount of risk involved and the effort required, certain conditions need to be set in order for team development to be effective:

1. Those in a leadership position (i.e., manager) must be committed and involved. Team building cannot take place in the absence of a formal team leader, nor can the leader maintain an indifferent or tongue-in-cheek attitude.
2. There must be a willingness on the part of the team leader to look at his or her own role in relation to the team.
3. There should be a high commitment on the part of all team members and a willingness to take 100% responsibility for making the effort work. Taking less than 100% responsibility leaves too many loopholes for members to take a "wait and watch the other guy" attitude.
4. There must be a commitment on the part of all team members to study their own process and to critique their own performance. These two activities are a never-ending process and continue throughout the life of the team.
5. Team building is not possible if there are no team (staff) meetings. Some work units operate by having the manager meet with his or her subordinates on an individual basis rather than having regular team meetings. This style of management allows no opportunity for team members to relate to each other as a group in more direct face-to-face interactions. Rather, they relate to each other through the medium of a manager.
6. Team-building activities are not limited to special sessions, retreats, or occasions when the consultant comes, but rather should take place on a day-to-day basis at work. Team members should have a commitment to put into practice what they learned at special sessions or retreats.

7. It should be understood that team building is not a one-shot process but rather a process of continuous diagnosis, action planning, implementation, and evaluation.

Generally speaking, team building involves several steps. The first step is making the initial contact between the consultant and the client (manager) to establish what assistance the client needs and how they are going to work together.

Second, the consultant may gather data about the team culture (how people work together, and the norms, values, beliefs, policies, and practices governing their behavior) to determine what the current state of the team is and in what direction changes need to be made in order to facilitate movement toward organizational objectives. Determining the current status of the team means that the traditions and norms by which the team is operating need to be made explicit.

Third, the data collected (diagnosis) are organized in terms of goals that the members of the team feel they need to achieve in order to improve their functioning as a team. A major aspect of the diagnosis is to look at norms governing team behavior to determine which ones are inhibiting or facilitating team effectiveness. This step may involve establishing a standard of excellence (criteria of effectiveness) along a number of behavioral and procedural dimensions against which to measure progress. These dimensions can be converted to goal statements reflecting how the team would like to see itself performing.

During the fourth step, concrete interventions are planned and implemented to achieve these goals. That is, action plans are developed to keep, modify, or drop old norms and/or initiate new norms that the team agrees to adopt.

Fifth, the results of the interventions are evaluated to measure the degree of goal achievement (how do you know the norm is operating; if so, to what extent, and are the results those that were anticipated?)

Finally, follow-up evaluations are instituted periodically to track progress and to provide ongoing diagnoses on which to base further interventions. Best learning will occur when a norm for ongoing self-evaluation becomes an integral part of the team's culture.

The total process, or parts of it, may repeat itself in a cyclical pattern, with objectives changing as the needs of the team change. It must be remembered that team development does not take place in isolation but must be related to other teams or groups in order to achieve the overall objectives of the organization in which the team is embedded. For additional reading, see Dyer (1987) and Reddy and Jamison (1988).

Note

1. Blake and Mouton (1968, pp. 97-107) found that when team members assess themselves without any structured way of doing so, they tend to base their perceptions on what they would like to see or believe and thus have an inflated evaluation of how they are operating. When team members can agree on what constitutes an ideal model of how to function and solve problems, they provide themselves with a "model of excellence" against which they can measure their own team behaviors. As a consequence, they can be more objective and realistic as to how they are doing now and to agree on how they would like to be working. Through this procedure, discrepancies become very evident and suggest starting points for team development.

What Is OD?

A basic assumption in most programs for change is that nobody works alone in an organization. Each of us is involved in daily interactions with other individuals. We belong to work units or teams (groups), and we participate in meetings for the purpose of planning work goals, receiving and giving information, making decisions, solving problems, and achieving many other objectives. In this process we attempt to satisfy our needs, not only to be a productive contributor to the organization's mission, but to meet our own needs for social interactions. Few, if any, formal educational experiences are organized to provide us with skills and understanding of complex human interactions and of being an effective member and leader of groups, teams, and organizations. The profession of OD is an attempt to work with both sides of the equation: personal and organizational needs.

OD, or, if you prefer, organizational improvement, is a planned effort to help people work and live together more effectively and productively, over time, in their organization. To live more effectively and productively involves:

- Increasing awareness of behaviors that help or hinder personal and organization development.
- Adopting ways of relating and doing the work that better integrate individual needs with organizational goals.
- Helping the organization to make better use of its human resources.
- Increasing members' participation in decisions that affect their work lives.
- Increasing individual members' trust in using themselves as a significant resource.
- Changing the organizational culture to reinforce these behavioral goals. This last item is not an easy task to accomplish.

These goals are achieved through the application of behavioral science research methods and theories adapted from the fields of psychology, sociology, education, and management.

OD involves several steps. First, the consultant makes the initial contact with the client to explore, clarify, and establish what assistance the client needs and how they are going to work together. The initial and subsequent interviews may also address who the client is (i.e., initial contact person, intermediate contacts, primary and ultimate client) (Schein, 1987). Second, on the basis of the early interviews with the client, the consultant may gather data about the culture of the client organization (how the people work together and the norms governing their behavior) to determine the state of the organization and some possible directions in which changes need to be made in order to facilitate movement toward organizational objectives. Third, the data are fed back to those members from whom it was collected. Members can then see to what extent their own perceptions agree or disagree with the perceptions of others. The feedback session can also give them a more "objective" sense of the organization's problem. Fourth, the data collected (diagnoses) are organized by the consultant and the members in terms of goals that the members of the client organization feel they need to achieve in order to improve their functioning as an organization. If the goals are general, they need to be restated in specific and measurable behavioral terms. During the fifth step, concrete interventions are planned and implemented to achieve these goals. Sixth, the interventions are evaluated to measure the degree of goal achievement. Timing of evaluation is important here. Last, follow-up evaluations are instituted periodically to track progress and to provide ongoing diagnoses on which to base further interventions. The extent to which the manager and his or her employees are directly involved in these seven steps depends upon what decisions were made in the first step. A major value of OD, however, is to involve the client in all steps. The total process, or parts of it, may repeat itself in a cyclical pattern, with objectives changing as the needs of the organization change.

Burke (1994) cited three criteria to be met before a change program can qualify as OD (p. 9):

1. The client "responds to an actual and perceived need for change" (Steps 3-7 above).
2. The consultant "involves the client in the planning and implementation of the change" (Steps 1-7).
3. The interventions "lead to change in the organization's culture" (Steps 6 and 7 may help to determine to what extent a cultural change has occurred).

Other approaches, (e.g., sociotechnical systems) share technologies with OD. They appear to be moving closer to each other. We will describe some of these systems. For our purposes, however, we will continue to use the term OD as a generic umbrella when addressing other technologies.

The term OD itself can get in the way of a fuller understanding of what OD is in that it is sometimes perceived by the client as separate from on-the-job issues and problems. That is, "When the consultant comes, it is OD time." When the consultant leaves, it is time to get back to dealing with "normal" work issues. What happens between consultant visits is defined as working on *real* job problems rather than OD. This dilemma constitutes a failure to see the continuity of the OD process and the need for fully integrating the OD effort with ongoing work issues.

In its broadest terms, any attempt to improve the organization through involving the clients in identifying problems, planning ways to deal with these problems, evaluating what was done, and assessing the extent to which the new behaviors have been adopted and affect the culture is OD.

Because we live in a state of continuous change, goals established today may be obsolete tomorrow. OD, therefore, is not a one-shot intervention by an outside consultant, but an ongoing, long-term, repetitive process in which management and others are trained to diagnose their organization or work unit, reevaluate their goals, plan ways to bring about needed change, and evaluate results.

Below are some statements that are typical of OD goals:

- OD attempts to integrate individual needs for growth with organizational goals. The assumption here is that an organization can achieve its goals more effectively if it takes into consideration and supports individual needs. These needs include the need to assume more responsibility for decisions that affect one's work life, to receive recognition for competency rather than on the basis of status, to have open communication with coworkers, and to be creative and contribute to problem solving.

- OD attempts to build into an organization some procedures that will be of long-term use in identification of internal problems and that will lead to a better quality of solutions for these problems.

- OD attempts to change systems toward being more open. That is, it tries to legitimatize self-examination that has been denied in the past and to open up areas to change that have not been previously open or have been considered "untouchable."

- To unfreeze, move, and refreeze systems, OD practitioners work on perceptions, feelings, relationships, attitudes, group norms, and communication skills among people at the top and middle of organizations.

- OD is a process of increasing awareness of implicit behavioral patterns that help and hinder development. Once organization members bring these patterns into conscious awareness, they can reinforce behaviors that help development and change behaviors that hinder it (Burke, 1994).

- OD "is a planned process of change in an organizational culture through the utilization of behavioral science technologies, research and theory" (Burke, 1994, p. 12).

- OD "is an organizational process for understanding and improving any and all substantive processes an organization may develop for performing any tasks and pursuing any objectives"—"a process for improving processes" (Vaill, 1989b, p. 261).

What is the history of OD?
When and where did it begin?

The field of OD did not begin as an integrated, coherent discipline. In the 1940s and 1950s, many behavioral scientists who were consulting with organizations developed their own systems of facilitating management development and organizational effectiveness. What they shared were democratic values in the workplace and a scientific ethos. Another common experience for many of them was their membership in the National Training Laboratories Institute of Applied Behavioral Science (NTL Institute). This institute grew out of workshops on race relations at the State Teachers College in New Britain, Connecticut, in 1946. The workshop staff and subsequent founders of NTL were Kurt Lewin, Ken Benne, Lee Bradford, and Ron Lippitt. The workshop format used small, low-structured groups, designated as *basic skills training groups* or *T-groups* (as they were later called), that focused their attention on here-and-now group dynamics.

The first public program based on this educational method using T-groups as the primary source of learning was instituted in 1947 at Gould Academy in Bethel, Maine. This technology was later applied to organizational settings. For example, we know that the group dynamics that occur, and are examined, in T-groups are present in all groups (work groups, school groups, social groups, therapy groups, etc.). The early consultants applied this learning to the work setting, where the dynamics of work teams at all levels could be studied for the effectiveness of operations (e.g., how decisions are made, how to balance maintenance behaviors with task functions, how to identify group norms and their effect on group behavior). This technology, however, ran into difficulties because it tended to isolate the in-house groups from their larger organizational setting. The primary elements that were transferred to organizations more successfully were the laboratory method of education (experiential learning) and the application of behavioral science methodologies. The NTL rosters from the 1960s read like a Who's Who of the behavioral sciences and appear in any history of OD: Chris Argyris, Bernard Bass, Richard Beckhard, Warren Bennis, Robert Blake, Michael Blansfield, Paul Buchanan, Warner Burke, Jerry Harvey, George Lehner, Ron Lippitt, Gordon Lippitt, Fred Massarick, Jane Mouton, Edgar Schein, Herbert Shepard, Warren Schmidt, Peter Vaill, Dale Zand. Other early members were well known in the mental health area of the behavioral sciences: James Bugenthal, Carl Rogers, and Irvin Yalom. It is important to note that Kurt Lewin died February 11, 1947, and never saw Bethel, Maine; nor was he present at the first public human interaction laboratory there the following summer. His concept of "action research" underlies all laboratory education and organization development. For a short history of the NTL Institute, see Weisbord (1987, pp. 99-104) and French and Bell (1990, pp. 24-32).

OD Values

What are some of the underlying and expressed values of OD?

Most of the OD values stem from the philosophical values of the laboratory method of learning and change (e.g., laboratory education, human interaction laboratory, human relations training, sensitivity training) and its roots in the behavioral sciences. As OD evolved out of the laboratory method, it carried with it the basic values related to human beings, learning, and change. These values are not rigidly formulated, but are held as guidelines to behavior. A caveat is noted here: People's values are more truly revealed in what they do than in what they say.

A basic value in which all other values are embedded is embodied by the terms *humanism* and *human rights*. Essentially, the humanistic value mandates that we guide our behaviors in a way that does not discount, diminish, or dehumanize any person or group.

Organizations are essentially networks of human relationships. Organizations do not exist outside of the people who constitute them. How these people work together affects the quantity and quality of the product. Most people working in OD consultation share some basic values that they feel are facilitative in helping people and organizations work more effectively. Some representative OD values follow:

Concept of People

1. People are basically healthy, self-motivated organisms who need to work and live in systems that respect them and their humanity.

2. People will support what they help create. They will be more highly invested and committed if they participate in decisions and in solving problems that affect their lives both in the community and at work.

3. People have growth needs that develop from infancy to maturity. These dimensions move from passivity to activity, dependence to independence, simple to complex behaviors, erratic short-term perspective to long-term perspective, subordinate position to equal or superordinate position, and lack of self-awareness to self-awareness and self-control (Argyris, 1957).

4. These growth needs are activated by a certain amount of psychological energy that exists in all individuals, and they will find some type of expression even when they are blocked. When not blocked or thwarted by community and organizational practices or norms that inhibit them, these growth tendencies will facilitate the development of healthy, mature, and self-actualizing individuals.

Values Reflected in How One Does OD

1. It is important to examine one's own values and the extent to which they are reflected in one's behavior.

2. It is important to accept values in others different from one's own and to deal with these value differences openly.

3. Interpersonal relations are as legitimate an area of organizational concern as is task performance.

4. To develop more interpersonal effectiveness, one needs to look at one's own leadership style and how it affects others.

5. OD is an ongoing process involving continuous diagnosis and concern for long-run effectiveness. It is not a quick fix for immediate results.

6. The process by which work is done, as well as the content of the work, is important. It is the process that is the primary concern of OD.

7. There is a commitment to learn about organizational dynamics and to put that learning to use (e.g., how the organization is affected by subgroups or subsystems from within and by the environment from without).

8. The personal and professional development of the OD consultant, like OD itself, is a never-ending, ongoing process.

Values supporting OD can also be categorized into three major concerns: scientific inquiry, the democratic process, and the helping relationship. Much of the material below is summarized from Benne (1975, pp. 24-55).

Concern for Science. The experiential learning or laboratory approach, or OD, places a high value on fully utilizing the concepts and methods of the social and behavioral sciences, particularly as they apply to the practical affairs of organizational life. Central to the scientific method are such values as objectivity, integrity, and the pursuit of information relevant to the issues, regardless of vested interests and political expediency. Thus decision making, problem solving, and change can be accomplished on the basis of objective evidence rather than emotionally derived notions that maintain a status quo. Even the term *laboratory* carries with it scientific implications and suggests experimental inquiry and methodologies derived from science.

Scientists have a moral obligation to consider all the facts in any problem situation. The person who is trying to make life a science must remember that people's feelings are also facts. In the laboratory of human relations, the attitudes and feelings of human beings must be taken into consideration and weighed with as much respect as one would treat any other type of data.

There is some evidence that the behavioral sciences and their attendant values are underutilized in such practical affairs of organizations as decision making, problem solving, and planning. Devotion to finding and facing facts, free and open communication of findings, and pursuit of objectivity appear to be neglected in the process of action decisions, in which efficiency, profitability, win/lose competition, and "tribal" offensive and defensive warfare tend to dominate.

Concern for Democracy. In many organizations, people are often remote from the point at which decisions are made that concern their lives. The remoteness removes them from responsible involvement in handling their own affairs and in managing their lives. Responsibility resides in the hands of others. The individual lapses into passivity and loses enthusiasm, involvement, and active participation in planning and executing personal goals.

The democratic process fosters responsible involvement in goal setting, decision making, and problem solving in the affairs that concern one's own work and life. This process also involves a commitment to collaborate with others in defining problems and in working through solutions. Furthermore, one needs to test one's own assumptions, biases, and values as they impinge on the problem-solving process. The democratic process also implies valuing evidence that is objective and relevant to the issues rather than personal or political points of view that run counter to the data.

For equality to have any meaning, people must see themselves as having reasonable control over their own fates rather than as being pawns to be moved about by superiors. They must feel they have the power to change their behavior and their working conditions and to assume full responsibility for the change and for the consequences. The management philosophy of OD must exemplify the democratic process, not only in manager/employee relationships but among managers themselves.

The job of managers is to create a climate that encourages self-expression, that makes it possible for employees to recognize and develop their assets, that enables them to feel they have something of value to contribute, and that allows them to participate in the creative and decision-making phases of their own work life. The task is one of freeing employees to realize their potential and to become less dependent, more responsible, and more capable of making contributions.

In many organizations, the concern for democracy is more honored than practiced. There is much lip service to the democratic ideal, but when the hard decisions are to be made, many managers find it easier to sidestep the employees and fall back on self-authorized decision making. The democratic process is often seen as impractical and a threat to power relations and the status quo. Unfortunately, many people in authority see the democratic approach as giving up power rather than investing it. In reality, managers do not give up power when they are sharing it. They can take it back any time they wish. The increasing size and complexity of organizations and the increasing remoteness of individuals from decision-making opportunities make responsible involvement difficult. These factors may increase the need to redefine democratic values operationally to make them more relevant to the demands of contemporary organizational life.

The innovators of the laboratory approach saw a considerable overlap between the scientific and democratic ethic. A reality orientation to addressing these problems is partly educational and partly reeducational in developing new perspectives and skills that are targeted more to current organizational issues.

Concern for the Values of the Helping Relationship. Values guide the behavior of the consultant (helping person) as well as the client (receiver of help). This relationship involves a joint commitment to the facilitation of learning and competence in the client (individual, group, or organization).

The keynote of group democratic action is collaboration with others in making decisions, providing helpful feedback, assisting others to express themselves, giving emotional support and acceptance, dealing more effectively with conflict and change, and improving the helping process itself. Managers and employees must become cooperatively interdependent. Each individual provides the type of assistance he or she is most qualified to give.

Each takes the assistance most appropriate to his or her needs. As groups or teams develop trust and confidence, the need for help is expressed more openly. OD practitioners and managers come to recognize that helping relationships are most effective and satisfying when the assistance offered does not encourage dependence but enables the receivers to work out the solution for themselves. In this way, clients and employees develop more confidence in their ability to cope with problems. They become more capable of contributing something worthwhile to the team and to the organization.

To help each other, OD consultants should be aware of different styles of helping and their consequences. They must also be sensitized to the barriers and difficulties of both giving and receiving help. A "helping relationship" considers the different purposes for seeking help and the types of communication involved in each helping situation.

Unfortunately, all clients do not come to us with open minds and open hearts. Many of them may have defensive postures toward receiving help. The resistance to receiving help may take many forms, both obvious and subtle. How can the consultant avoid being drawn into these defensive maneuvers and still be helpful? Are the helpers sufficiently self-aware and comfortable with themselves not to be threatened by a manipulative client?

> What orientation might enable the helping professions to find common ground in their specialized efforts to help clients? The innovators of laboratory training found such an orientation in the generalized conception of the change agent—an agent committed to help others in improving their abilities to cope effectively with change and conflict. (Benne, 1975, p. 44)

Are OD values appropriate to every organization, community, and nation? Are they appropriate to organizations with clandestine missions? What to do or how to practice OD when the client's value system does not match, is not congruent with, or is opposed to OD values? Can OD still be done?

In countries in which the prevailing political atmosphere is democratic, OD values would just be an extension of that climate. In cultures that are highly autocratic and in which social position is governed by caste or class systems, OD values may not be accepted and may be seen as inappropriate. If the client system's values are not congruent with OD values, it may be useful to help the client group make their philosophical assumptions clear and their values explicit concerning a number of human issues. The client group can then examine what types of managerial behaviors stem from their values and the consequences, short and long term, of these behaviors on productivity and morale. In this way, the consultant can apply OD methods without imposing his or her OD values. Whatever the client group discovers after an examination of the consequences of their values will determine whether they need to change their culture. If they decide to move in the direction of change, the goals may be more consistent with OD values. In this manner, the client, not the consultant, makes the decision to change. The consultant can then continue to practice OD.

What do values have to do with OD practice? Is OD value neutral? Would consultants compromise their work by introducing values? Are values another name for biases?

As has been demonstrated in the value statements above, OD is not value neutral. Values give meaning to what a person does and guide behavior. When consultants or any individuals are clear about their values, they are much more aware when they are behaving in a way consistent or inconsistent with their values. Behaving in ways inconsistent with one's values creates a sense of dissonance and tension within oneself. Consultants' behavior, what they say and do, reflects their values. It is only when they try to impose their values on others that they may compromise their work. To impose values is like saying "my values are good and yours are bad." Burke (1994) felt he had no right to impose his values on a client system.

> For me to assume that I can act as a value-free consultant, however, is pure nonsense. It is most important for me to work toward as much clarity of my values as possible and to declare these values relatively early in the consultant-client relationship. Most are clear anyway if the client has paid any attention to my behavior and to my recommendations. (p. 199)

In a way, values are biases. If people's values are consistent with democratic values, they are partial to systems and groups that espouse these ideals. To be partial toward something is to be biased. It is only when we are unaware of our biases (values) that we may act ineffectively with whomever we are involved. Unfortunately, however, the term *bias* has a negative connotation, and we like to think of ourselves as having "values," not "biases."

Why is it important to examine our values when doing OD? How is OD related to individual values?

When managers or consultants examine their values, they are much more likely to be clear about them. Clarity about their values enables them to assess more effectively how values affect their work and their behavior with client systems. Individuals are also better able to discover to what extent OD values are similar to or different from their own personal values.

Some consultants will not work with systems they see as militaristic (armed services, police, extreme political right) because of the discrepancy between their own personal values and what they perceive as the values in these other systems. In many of these systems, however, there is movement toward a modified form of democracy in at least parts of the system. The consultant who will not work with these systems gives up the opportunity to influence them in a more humanistic direction. In the final analysis it is the consultants' choice. They know themselves better than others know them, and know better what choices are best for them. They should feel free to choose or not choose any options before them.

To what extent are OD values consistent with maximum profit making?

Today, the expression *maximum profit making* is interpreted (or misinterpreted) as something against the public interest. The lack of trust in "big business" is nourished by associated publicized descriptions such as "profit in our time," "corporate greed," "government bailout," "learned incompetence," and "secret agenda." If maximum profit making means sacrificing long-term for short-term quick profits, again, the answer is that the values are inconsistent. "Profit in our time" is a self-serving philosophy not attuned to the long-term vision of the organization. If maximum profit making is equivalent to large bonuses and salary increases to corporate officers at the expense of employee benefits and incentives, the OD values are not being represented. The loyalty of the employees to the organization cannot be expected by management when such discrepancies in the organizational reward system exist.

Profit making itself is not necessarily inconsistent with OD values. In this highly competitive business world, however, it would be naive to expect organizations not to compete with each other. To gain a competitive edge may be critical to the life or possible death of an organization. How does an organization compete and grow and at the same time operate in a way consistent with OD values? Many organizations are realizing that their own health and long-term growth are dependent on a more future-oriented management of their own resources, a more sensitive consideration of their most important resource—people—and a more equitable distribution of their rewards.

To what extent are OD values consistent with modern management?

From the list previously presented concerning underlying and expressed values, it would appear that many OD values are consistent with modern managerial values, at least their expressed values. The difficulty lies in how those values are implemented in behavior. For example, some managers may profess a belief in the democratic process in terms of decision making, shared resources, and problem solving. In terms of how they really behave, however, they actually operate in a very autocratic way, making unilateral decisions, distributing resources according to position and affiliation rather than need, and showing more concern for tasks, procedures, and material support than for morale or people problems. The consistency in values may also vary among managers within an organization, depending upon their attitude toward learning and the breadth of their view of management. With the influx of team-oriented management, modern managers do see the value of participative involvement of employees. The true test of their values, however, comes in times of crises: Do managers revert back to more autocratic control and self-authorized decision making as a way to solve problems?

To what extent are OD values consistent with a large organization (e.g., a bureaucracy)?

Most large organizations have two systems operating: a formal and an informal one. The informal system develops values that are not always consonant with the values or goals of the formal organization. Some of these values are "Always protect yourself (CYA)," "Never volunteer," "Play the game if you want to get along or get ahead," and "Don't clarify the issue, otherwise you might have to live with it." The values of the formal system may vary somewhat, depending upon the situation and the time. For instance, values may be more autocratic during times of financial stress, crises, or war, and less so during times of financial security, tranquillity, or peace. The more autocratic an organization's management philosophy, the more dependent an employee will be on the informal system. Traditionally, in bureaucratic organizations there has been a tendency to suppress individuality in favor of group or organizational norms that stress conformity of behavior and submission to authority. Many large organizations today are in a healthy struggle of redefining their own value system and looking at alternative ways of managing. This self-exploration and assessment is consistent with OD values. Currently, OD practitioners are moving toward the effective management of large-scale organization change. This movement will involve greater emphasis on "culture, values, key leadership acts (providing vision and clear sense of direction), the reward system and management/executive programs" (Burke, 1994, p. 200).

Does OD lead to development of alternative systems to the formal administrative structure?

To the extent that the administrative structure does not involve shared decision making at all levels and is not responsive to the needs of its individual members or the current social pressures, alternative systems may develop. Some organizations, with their emphasis on developing a more democratic organization, may already represent an alternative or supplementary system to the traditional authoritative structure. There are influences within today's society that tend to move organizations in the direction of more participative management. At present, the focus is on trying to make the administration more responsive in terms of a more humane approach to individual employees, a greater recognition of their individual needs, and a greater recognition of how these needs can be integrated with, and contribute to, organizational goals. We can reiterate Bennis's (1966) vision of values as expressed in Weisbord (1987): "an integration of science and democracy aimed at flatter organizations and more egalitarian relationships" (p. 255). The increasing utilization of work teams, participative groups, group problem-solving sessions, quality circles, and quality of work life may indeed be moving organizations toward Bennis's vision.

Some General Questions

Is OD a philosophy, a way of thinking, an art, a science, or all of the above?

OD has a philosophical basis and values rooted in the democratic and scientific ethos. The OD consultant thinks primarily in terms of process: that is, how things are done, how people relate to each other, how decisions are made, and how involved people are in those decisions that affect their work situation. It is also an art in that it encourages creativity, atypical ways of approaching problems, and utilization of the resources of the right side of the brain as well as the left side. More recently, other philosophical systems such as Eastern mysticism and spirituality have crept into OD. Vaill (1989a) had a chapter titled "Taoistic Management: 'Composedly they went and came.'" He addressed the writings of Lao Tzu, which are as appropriate to today's organizations as they were 2,500 years ago. Lao Tzu's concept of leadership is reflected in the following quote (Bynner, 1962):

> *A leader is best*
> *When people barely know that he exists.*
> *Not so good when people obey and acclaim him,*
> *Worst when they despise him.*
> *Fail to honor people,*
> *They fail to honor you.*
> *But of a good leader,*
> *Who talks little,*

> *When his work is done,*
> *His aim fulfilled,*
> *They will say,*
> *"We did this ourselves."*
> Lao Tzu (604?-500 B.C.),

Other titles currently in business sections of book stores are *The Tao of Leadership* (Heider, 1985), *The Tao of Management* (Messing, 1989), *The Tao of Psychology* (Bolen, 1979), *The Tao of Negotiation* (Edelman & Crain, 1993), *The Tao of Time* (Hunt & Hait, 1990), and *The Tao at Work* (Herman, 1994). In his chapter "The Requisites of Visionary Leadership," Vaill (1989a) addressed spirituality, which he defined for himself as "the search for a deeper experience of the spirit of various kinds that one can feel stirring within" (p. 213), and stated that in reference to leadership, "Vision that is not centered in a profound spirituality is nothing more that a pictorial 'might-be' of an organization's future" (p. 223). There is and has been for several years a resurgence of Eastern and Western mysticism and spirituality in the behavioral sciences and mental health (see also Chapter 3 on values). These ancient codes of effective personal and leadership behavior have much to offer in today's social and organizational life; to ignore them as not relevant to our times is to be socially and philosophically myopic.

Is OD another name for "sensitivity training"?

No. There is a relationship, however, which is described somewhat differently by different OD consultants:

- Sensitivity training is a specific application of behavioral science that addresses itself to individuals' needs to become more effective in their interpersonal relations and to further their own personal growth. These individual needs may include upgraded skills in observing interpersonal and group dynamics, keener awareness of oneself and one's impact on others in any given group or meeting, sharper ability to communicate effectively, and greater openness to receiving feedback about one's own behavior. OD, however, is concerned primarily with organizations and organizational needs. When individual and organizational needs coincide or are in conflict, sensitivity training may be part of an OD effort.
- Sensitivity training and OD are somewhat related in that they both are applications of behavioral science.

- To the degree that sensitivity training deals with interpersonal competence and group and leadership skills, it may be used to "unfreeze" an organization in the early stages of OD, or to prepare people for OD work.

How is OD related to, or different from, training?

Training, in general, as distinct from sensitivity training, may be a part of OD when the goals of OD indicate a need to help people develop skills and competencies that would facilitate movement toward desired goals or changes. Training, in general, may include workshops and seminars on managerial leadership skills, conflict management, problem solving, strategic planning, and other similar topics. For example, changes in the way managers function both alone and in work groups may be an OD goal. To improve the skills necessary for these changes may necessitate training. Again, OD is geared primarily toward the organization rather than the individual and consists mainly of consultation rather than training.

Is OD another name for "soft management"?

No. OD may have gotten this label in some organizations because of the importance it gives to feelings and other human values such as individuals' importance in their own right as well as a part of an organizational team. In contrast to soft management, OD is very demanding on those who manage. The values of OD require that there be high concern for work accomplishment as well as for employee needs, that individuals assume responsibility for their own behavior, that they be open to challenge and feedback from others, that they be accepting of differences between themselves and others and be willing to work with them, that they be open to a wide range of management styles and use these appropriately, and that they work effectively with others from their own base of competence rather than from a position of status. If OD is effective, it identifies and utilizes all resources, a difficult enough task in itself, and is certainly not to be equated with soft management.

Does OD mean
participative management?

There are two general responses among OD consultants: One is "yes" and the other is "not necessarily." The "yes" group states that OD means participative management (PM) because it values people's participation in decision making and their contribution to problem solving. In this respect, much decision making is moved down to where the action is rather than remaining at a management level that is remote from the actual work situation. The philosophy reflected in the "yes" statements is that "people will support what they help create." The concepts of OD and PM do not mean that there are no lines of formal authority, communication, responsibility, and accountability. The concept of PM is greatly misunderstood and frequently downgraded because of failures due to poor conceptualization and mismanagement of the effort.

The "not necessarily" group sees OD and PM as similar when PM is the style indicated as the most appropriate for the situation. In other words, in OD the nature of the situation or task determines which style of management or leadership is most effective. In some cases, it may be appropriate to make autocratic or unilateral decisions. The important factor here is helping the leader be "authentic" and effective in his or her style (i.e., to use the style that is most natural to the manager and with which he or she functions best, and to be aware of the consequences of his or her choice and its impact on others).

How does OD differ from
just good management practices?

Good management practices are similar to OD if they involve the following:

- A commitment to utilize all resources available, particularly all human resources
- Clear and explicit assumptions of management
- Programming that is planned, anticipating some measure of predictability and change
- A readiness to deal with and to integrate the emotional side of organizational life
- A perspective that views the organization as a total system made up of interrelated subsystems and influenced by its environment (e.g., adjacent systems)

- Reflection of a set of values or a philosophy rather than a set of techniques that have some type of sanction as being "good"

Does OD have anything to do with the "product" or the manager's "work," or does it just deal with interpersonal relations?

OD has a great deal to do with the product or one's work. The better individuals feel about themselves, their colleagues, their job, and the organization, the more effectively they will work and the higher investment they will have in the product. OD is an effort to give integrity and worth to an individual within an organization. One measure of a successful OD program may be increased quantity and/or quality of output (work), or the degree to which organizational goals or missions are achieved (see the section in Chapter 6 on quality of work life).

Organizations do not exist independently of people, nor can organizational goals be accomplished except by and through people. A basic assumption of OD is that productivity increases as the organizational process (i.e., how people work together) receives due consideration. OD tends to reduce friction in the interpersonal machinery so that time and energy can be productively focused on real issues and not be diverted into nonproductive interpersonal areas like competitiveness, bickering, and indirect communication. Interpersonal relationships are relevant to the extent that they are affecting the organization's work. A major focus of OD may be to clarify the nature of the interpersonal relationships that already exist and to bring about some understanding as to how these relationships can inhibit or facilitate the achievement of organizational goals.

How long does OD take? Can it be done quickly? How do you make OD a sustainable improvement?

In OD there are no quick fixes. The preceding statement is apparent in our definitions of OD. Indeed, some consultants will not start an OD program if there is not a commitment from the client for a period of time sufficient to complete the project. To produce a change in the organization's culture (one of Burke's criteria), we have to address facets of that culture that may involve long-standing, habitual, and ingrained patterns of behavior. These behaviors are supported by group norms, beliefs, attitudes, and historical precedents. The consultant and the client identify a value that they would like to see inculcated into the organization: for example, involving subordinates in decisions that affect their work situation. This value may run counter to more autocratic managers' style of making decisions and cannot be addressed directly. Managers must learn to behave in a way consistent with the value. Furthermore, they must practice the new behavior. If the new behavior is reinforced (rewarded) by more effective decision making, it then results in a change of attitude. The change of attitude and its consequential behaviors then become valued and are consistent with the targeted value originally identified by the consultant and the client. When the OD program involves several targets for change or different values to be adopted, the process becomes more complicated, increasing possibilities for resistance to change. Many of us have had the experience of trying to change a behavior but have run into self-defeating counter-behaviors (our own resistance to change). For example, losing weight, giving up smoking, and less impulsive spending are goals that may be very difficult to achieve and may take considerable time, effort, and monitoring before any progress can be noted. Any behaviors that have been long ingrained and are habitual may have reinforcing elements that increase the resistance to change (e.g., it may be more comfortable and less threatening to maintain an individual or organizational status quo). This change process does not occur overnight. Why, then, should a change process involving many diverse people take a shorter period of time? Again, any effort for sustainable improvement must include continuous diagnosis, planning, intervention, and evaluation until the process becomes an integral part of organizational life. OD is a process that is ongoing; there is really no end point. And again, practice is the critical ingredient. Alfred Adler once said that insight alone is not sufficient for change to occur; change requires practice.

How much time does it take to change an organization's culture?

Organizational culture, as we have described in Chapter 1, is a highly complex phenomenon. When we talk about cultural change, are we alluding to behavioral changes of the organization's members or changes in the organization's values and assumptions? Are we focusing on the total organization or on one aspect or subsystem? Are we looking at some of the other factors to be considered in changing a culture, such as the age of the organization, its size and complexity, the nature of the environment in which it operates, and how ingrained the cultural assumptions are? Schein (1985) addressed the complexity not only of defining *culture* but of assessing cultural change. He also questioned the necessity of cultural change, in many situations, in order for an OD program to be successful.

The culture of a subsystem (e.g., a management team) may be relatively easy to assess and change. This change will depend, of course, on how many of the criteria in Chapter 1 on team building have been met. The change from a manager-dominated to a team mode of operation can be measured periodically throughout the team's life (see Chapter 10 on evaluation) by using instruments similar to those described in this book's appendixes. Before assessing the team's levels of functioning or mode of operation, criteria for success or goal achievement should be decided upon. The time span for change and maintenance of the change may be relatively short.

For larger, more complex systems, the time span for whatever cultural elements have been selected for change may be several years. Some consultants will not work with an organization unless it commits itself for a minimum of 5 years to an OD program. Indeed, some cultural changes may not become evident or measurable for several years. To expect measurable changes earlier may have a negative impact on an OD program that is actually working, but moving at a slow, steady pace. Unfortunately, in today's rapidly changing business world, many managers may not have the patience needed for slower-paced change and may push the consultant for more immediate results. To avoid this pressure, the consultant and the client at the front end of contracting will have to make some realistic time considerations and decide on time points at which change will be measured.

How do I know if an approach is OD or something else? Can you do OD without labeling it? Is it another name for "good" values and common sense?

In order to distinguish OD from something else, we would have to say that OD was a highly integrated, coherent, and identifiable approach to helping organizations become more effective. We cannot say this. Earlier in this chapter we compared OD with other approaches, describing differences and similarities. In Chapter 2, "What Is OD?", we defined *OD* and several criteria to help identify change projects as OD programs. Using these criteria as guidelines may help the manager determine that what he or she is doing is primarily OD, although other systems may be present, at least in part. Purity of concepts in this field is difficult to find. Part of the confusion, as we mentioned earlier, comes from the technologies and values OD shares with other approaches to organizational change. In many cases the overlap is considerable, and differences are more apparent than real. For example, team development, a consensus model for decision making, participative groups, and the concept of quality of work life may be common to many systems. In addition, these efforts may be only part of an OD program. As to whether OD is another name for "good" values and common sense, we certainly hope that the response to that question is adequately demonstrated throughout this book.

Is OD linear or nonlinear?

This question appears to stem from early psychological theory or from the field of physics. OD includes both linear and nonlinear thinking. Linear thinking implies that A is the cause of B, which is the cause of C: $A \rightarrow B \rightarrow C$, and, in reverse, that C is caused by B, which is caused by A. An example of linear thinking might be illustrated by a production line: A speedup in production in Department A causes a speedup or breakdown in Department B, which in turn affects the final phase of production in Department C.

In nonlinear thinking, A can cause, or influence directly, B, C, and D, or, in reverse, B, C, and D can cause A:

This process was identified early in psychoanalysis by Sigmund Freud in his concept of multiple cause and multiple effect. In OD systems thinking, a change in any part of a system can affect other or all parts of the system (nonlinear thinking). In Kurt Lewin's field theory (Lewin, 1935; Marrow, 1969), individuals operate in a field of forces that affects their behavior at any given moment. Some of these forces are internal (e.g., intelligence, values, motivation, state of health), and some are external (e.g., work situation, work associates, family, the economy). A change in one internal force (health) might affect job performance, relationships with others, finances, or concept of self. A change in one external force (termination of employment) might affect several of one's internal forces (e.g., outlook on life, financial status, feelings about oneself as a competent worker, self-esteem, relations with family), as well as some of the external forces cited above. By identifying many of the forces in one's life space, it is possible to analyze them and assess their impact on one's life (force field analysis).

It is important to recognize and utilize both ways of thinking and not to exclude one or the other prematurely in one's approach to organizational problem solving. In other words, keep your options open.

What is the future of OD?

The future of OD looks promising. How viable it will be depends upon many factors internal and external to the organizations themselves. The following questions are derived from French and Bell (1990) and Burke (1994):

- How accurately do OD efforts reflect the perceptions, concerns, and aspirations of participating members?
- How successful are OD practitioners in bringing about congruence with other programs aimed at organization improvement (e.g., job redesign, MBO, self-managed groups, QWL)?
- To what extent will OD theorists and practitioners develop new conceptual models appropriate to address contemporary problems?
- To what extent will these theorists and practitioners add clarity and focus to the field?
- To what extent will quality research illuminate the effectiveness of various intervention strategies?
- To what extent will theorists and practitioners retain and build on the insights of the past?

Burke saw OD as having "a bright future" (1994, p. 199). In his analysis,

"Societal and corporate trends are converging more with OD values and with what OD practitioners have to offer. . . . [The] quality movement, to be successful, is highly dependent on effective process, and process is the OD practitioner's most important product." (p. 199)

"We clearly have a set of standard tools that effectively address small to medium sized problems in organizations today." (p. 200)

"OD practitioners are beginning to face in another direction. . . . We are on the threshold of a paradigm for the effective management of large scale organizational change." (p. 200)

"We are beginning to understand much more clearly what the primary levers are for initiating and implementing organizational change, levers such as culture, value, key leadership acts (providing a vision and clear sense of direction), the reward system, and management/executive programs." (p. 200)

In summary, OD as a viable profession for the future is supported by the following:

- Grounding in the behavioral sciences and organizational theory
- An ever-expanding body of literature addressing theory and practice of OD
- A body of professionals who are committed to conceptualizing and developing theories as a basis on which to practice OD
- A body of professionals who are devoted to research for theory building and evaluation of the effectiveness of OD interventions
- A body of professionals who are willing to monitor and or confront unethical practices and practitioners whose primary motive is financial over and above OD values

The last item is concerned about the development of a negative image of OD brought on by practitioners who descend upon groups and organizations with their "bag of interventions" unsupported by theory and research. These consultants implement OD techniques and programs without adequate diagnoses or familiarity with organizational processes. In other words, they bypass most of what we have been addressing under "What Is OD?" (Chapter 2) and "What Are the Underlying and Expressed Values of OD?" (Chapter 3).

Is OD only for growth, or can it be used during periods of cutback? What is OD's position on downsizing and layoffs?

When we think of OD, it is usually in terms of increasing effectiveness and productivity and of developing human resources to enhance the organization's growth. *Development, productivity, effectiveness, growth, responsibility,* and *participation* are the key words. When an organization is downsizing and laying off personnel, how does OD address these issues? How the organization manages this process is where OD philosophy and values play a significant role. In the days before and immediately after World War II, many employees found a "pink slip" in their pay envelope. That notice was the only preparation for facing immediate unemployment. Even today there are glaring examples of firing with very little or no forewarning, as when owners of professional sports teams fire coaches, managers, and players.

Today there are massive layoffs. Large organizations that were once thought to be impervious to the vacillations of the world economy (e.g., General Motors, U.S. Steel) are closing plants and terminating thousands of employees. Downsizing and its consequential terminations of employees requires, if done humanely, OD processes such as diagnosing, planning, goal setting, and implementation. Part of the goal setting may involve employee counseling, vocational skill reassessment, occupational information, and future planning. For example, an OD consultant may work with the organization to set up a series of workshops, bringing in resources from the community to address financial planning, life goals, and career planning and employment opportunities locally and elsewhere. This type of exit planning would be an OD intervention. OD values are highly humanistic and are concerned with the well-being of the individual as well as the organization.

When is OD not needed?

When the organization and its culture do not need any change, then OD is not indicated. Many efforts for change in parts of an organization use such OD techniques as team building, feedback sessions, and off-site meetings, but that does not mean the organization is involved in OD.

There are indicators that are observable when an organization or an OD program is working effectively. Some of these are obvious and easy to measure. Some are more subtle and difficult to detect. The following list is not all-inclusive, but suggestive of a well-functioning OD effort. It can also describe an organization that does not need OD.

- Increased energy, enthusiasm, self-esteem, and revitalization of people within the organization
- Greater job satisfaction, more commitment to goals of organization, higher morale among employees
- Reduced turnover, absenteeism, and waste
- Growth (broadening) in concept of work, more flexible role definition
- Development of new programs and/or means for dealing with relevant mission issues
- Greater demands being made on the organization where none were being made before

- Better communication among managers, between managers and superiors, and between managers and subordinates

What are the signs that an organization needs an OD program or that OD is not working? The flip side of the previous list would obviously be included in this list. Burke (1994) cited a few indicators:
- The same problems keep recurring. As soon as one problem is addressed, another pops up. Managers are engaged in putting out brushfires.
- Many efforts have been tried to increase productivity, but none work.
- Morale is low and the cause is unclear.

Other signs are:

- Closed communication, continued dependency on rumors, and a sense of isolation from one another and from other parts of the system
- Climate of distrust, a greater felt need to protect oneself, less sharing
- Apathy, resistance to change, very little innovation and risk taking
- Avoidance of conflict and very little commitment to dealing with differences openly
- Decision making not shared, or prolonged agonizing over decisions with very little implementation
- Little or no ownership of the OD program or of the problems currently plaguing the organization

Does OD include systems thinking? Is it fixated only on small-systems change? How does environmental context affect OD applications?

Organizations are total systems consisting of several interdependent or interlocking subsystems. What happens in one subsystem affects other subsystems. The concept of interdependent systems has been used in subatomic physics and family systems theory for many years. In physics, everything is related to everything else. Subatomic particles "come into being and are observed only in relationship to something else. They do not exist as independent 'things'" (Wheatley, 1992). In families, what happens to one individual is determined by and affects every other member of the family. The family is an organization, and individual family members are the subsystems.

Several subsystems have been identified in organizations by different authors. Although there is considerable overlap, there are also some differences. Albrecht (1983) identified four, and French and Bell (1990) cited six subsystems. Current OD thinking is aware of the interdependence of an organization's subsystems even though the practitioner may be working on one subsystem. In addition, some practitioners may see their task as dealing only with the human/social subsystem. In this sense, the consultant's focus is on small-systems change. More recently, however, total and large-system OD is becoming increasingly the target of organizational improvement. This approach to the total organization obviously requires a systems focus. The following subsystems integrate Albrecht (1983) and French and Bell (1990).

Goal Subsystem. The goal subsystem consists of interrelated superordinate goals or objectives that make up the organization's mission statement. Important parts of the goal system are the subunit or program goals, which arise from and act interdependently with overall goals. How these goals interrelate can be a source of tension. The technical subsystems stem largely from the goal subsystem (French & Bell, 1990).

Human or Social Subsystem. The human or social subsystem is the area traditionally addressed by OD. It consists of people in the organization, how they work together, and their roles and relationships to one another. Included in this area are norms governing behavior, how authority and status are addressed, values, and ways in which performance is rewarded or punished. Individual and team development and leadership are three of the targets for attention. French and Bell (1990) subdivided this subsystem into four aspects: skills and abilities, leadership philosophy and style, a formal system, and an informal subsystem (see Chapter 1 on organization culture, which describes formal and informal subsystems).

Technical or Technological Subsystem. The technical or technological subsystem includes the tools, machines, procedures, methods, and technical knowledge. It is mainly concerned with the technical resources necessary to produce the product or service. Where people play a role, it is primarily in terms of their task functions and technical expertise. The two subsystems, the social and the technical, and their integration are the primary concerns of the sociotechnical system for improving organizations.

Task Subsystem. The task subsystem comprises the subdivision of the work to be accomplished by the members of the organization. It consists of the smaller units of tasks and subtasks needed to produce the end product. These tasks are highly dependent upon the technical subsystem.

Administrative Subsystem. The administrative subsystem reflects how information is distributed in the organization. It includes the people responsible for moving the information along the paths through which information flows, and policies, procedures, and reports that are critical to the operation of the organization. This communication subsystem is distinct from and a level above the subsystem that disseminates technical information (Albrecht, 1983).

Strategic Subsystem. The strategic subsystem concerns the management aspect of the organization. Individuals in this subsystem have formal leadership roles. They range from the CEO to the lowest level of supervisors. The features of this system include the chain of command, who reports to whom, where power lies, and the planning process and procedures used in governing the organization (Albrecht, 1983). This subsystem appears to overlap with the human/social subsystem.

Structural Subsystem. The structural subsystem consists of units, departments, services, and divisions that are grouped according to tasks to be performed and the design of the work flow. Included in this subsystem are work rules, authority systems, and procedures and practices relative to communicating, planning, coordination, control, and decision making. The technical, task, and structural subsystems are obviously highly interdependent (French & Bell, 1990).

External Interface Subsystem. The external interface subsystem consists of the environmental context in which the organization exists. It involves gathering data through market or public relation surveys, selecting and hiring personnel, purchasing material, advertising, public relations, lobbying, pollution control, and so on. In summary, this subsystem involves responses to external demands. The interface problems with the external environment are critical to the organization's survival (French & Bell, 1990). This particular subsystem was not included in Albrecht's four, which may mean that he was focusing only on the internal organization. The other subsystems identified by French and Bell (goal, task, and structural) can easily be integrated with Albrecht's administrative and strategic subsystems.

The question of how environmental context affects OD applications is addressed by our description of the external interface subsystem. Organizations cannot operate in isolation. Not only is the immediate environmental context important, but the global economy and foreign competition and cooperation can no longer be minimized. With the onslaught of foreign investment and buyouts, we are fast becoming a consumer, not a producer, nation. By broadening its perspective, OD needs to develop new concepts and models relevant to international organizational relationships. Historically, OD has moved from small-group dynamics to team building and small-systems change to intergroup interdepartmental relations to total organizational focus to interorganizational and international relations.

Is OD focused on implementing decisions, or can it play a major role in the development of strategic planning, corporate restructuring, futuring, and policy?

In Chapter 4, we addressed the expanding role of OD into the areas noted in the above question. Integrating these areas into an OD program would be part of a second phase after Phase 1 has been completed. Phase 1 would include an extensive diagnosis, feedback of data, problem identification and discussion, and action planning.

Once these other areas and their methodologies are included as an adjunctive system, the OD practitioner may then be a process consultant to look at the ways in which these systems operate (e.g., make decisions, solve problems, utilize resources, plan strategies). The role of the consultant in working with these other systems would, of course, entail mutual agreement. Again, it should be reiterated, no system (sub- or total) within an organization operates without a process. It is in this area (process) that the OD practitioner has the most to offer.

What are the limitations of OD? Where does it need to be coupled with other methodologies to be effective?

Until recently, OD tended to limit itself to interpersonal transactions, group or team processes, and intergroup (interdepartmental) dynamics. Essentially, OD focused on how people related to each other, how groups or work teams functioned, and how work units, departments, and services worked with one another. All of this activity was for the purpose of maintaining high morale and increasing productivity in the service of the organization's mission. This human factor emphasis stemmed primarily from the behavioral science application and the professional backgrounds of most of the early OD practitioners in psychology, sociology, and cultural anthropology, with their emphasis on action research. Currently, OD practitioners are paying more attention to role clarification, goal setting, strategic planning, and modification of structure and pay systems (French & Bell, 1990). They are also becoming more attentive to task functions, technological, financial, and structural aspects of organizations and their interdependencies not only with each other but with the people involved in their management. In addition, formerly, practitioners limited themselves to small-systems change. This focus is broadening to larger, more complex systems. There are still limits to what an OD program can do, and it must, at times, rely on other methodologies. French and Bell (1990) believed that these other technologies could be integrated with OD after the first phase (diagnosis, data feedback, problem discussion, and action planning) was completed. During a second phase, other resources could be identified as needed and coupled with the OD program. In these programs, OD practitioners would, of course, acknowledge their limitations and utilize these other resources (e.g., corporate planning, human resource management, labor relations, compensation, clinical psychology, management information systems, and industrial engineering). An OD program that does not take into consideration personnel or human resources is asking for trouble. These departments are intimately involved with the people in the organization, and their support (or involvement in the second phase) and contribution help pave the way for an effective program. If a plant is unionized, support by the union is also vital. Unions can block or even sabotage an OD program that may involve union members. Labor relations presents another opportunity for OD practitioners. Other methodologies, such as job description clarification, vocational and career counseling, employee assistance programs, and assessment of the impact of visual display panels, lighting, noise factors, and other physical work-environment conditions (human factors engineering), do not usually come under the purview of OD. There are some exceptions. Fred Steele (1973) was one of the early practitioners who included physical settings in his OD consulting. One of the purposes of his book was "to indicate ways in which physical environmental changes can be used as a means for starting or supporting social system changes" (p. 4). Some of these physical factors may include location, size, accessibility, lighting, windows, privacy, and, of course, status of office space and meeting or conference rooms.

OD Intervention

Interventions can range in scope from a simple question or an initial interview between a consultant and a client to a massive and complicated effort to change an organization's culture. "Even the consultant's presence is an intervention in that it sends a message to the organization that some one there has perceived a problem that warrants the presence of a consultant" (Schein, 1987, p. 31).

According to Argyris (1970), "To intervene is to enter into an ongoing system of relationships, to come between or among persons, groups, or objects for the purpose of helping them" (p. 15). There is an important assumption in the definition that the system exists independently of the intervenor. There is also an important assumption, when the intervention is based on OD philosophy, that the intervention is to assist or facilitate the organization to accomplish some change effort and not to coerce them to do what the intervenor wishes them to do.

French and Bell (1990) saw OD interventions as

> sets of structured activities in which selected organizational units (target groups or individuals) engage in a task or a sequence of tasks where the task goals are related directly or indirectly to organizational improvement. Interventions constitute the action thrust of organization development; they make things happen and are "what's happening." (p. 113)

Interventions can focus on an individual (coaching, sending a manager to a training event), groups (team building, survey feedback, retreats, strategic planning), departments or subsystems (data collection, diagnosis and problem-solving workshops, all-day confrontation meetings in which employees diagnose and present issues to management to address), or the total organization (strategic planning, survey feedback, assessing the process or restructuring, changing the culture around certain problem areas). When interventions are planned to deal with surface issues or manifest variables (e.g., skill development), they are called *phenotypic*. When the purpose is to tap underlying variables or root problems (e.g., norms, basic assumptions and beliefs), these interventions are referred to as *genotypic* (Argyris, 1970, p. 278). These two levels reflect the depth at which problems and goals are formulated. Genotypic interventions provide a more useful and complete understanding. There are several ways of classifying interventions that are beyond the scope of this answer. The interested reader may want to proceed further with the following authors: French and Bell (1990), Blake and Mouton (1964, 1976, 1983), Argyris (1970, 1993), and Schmuck and Miles (1971).

We need to remember that an OD intervention does not constitute an OD program. It may be only part of an OD program in progress (see definitions and criteria in Chapter 2). What is the best OD intervention? Obviously, one that is successful. An OD intervention has a better chance of success when it is relevant to the problems identified, when it is tied to some theoretical rationale, when it involves the client(s) in the planning, and when the nature of its execution is consistent with the values of OD.

How do you match an OD diagnosis with an intervention? What are the criteria for selecting an OD intervention? What are the conditions necessary to support an OD intervention? What is the best OD intervention?

We need to repeat the guideline that an OD intervention or event does not mean that an OD program is in progress. Many OD interventions may be limited to specific segments of the organization and may not involve the total system. We also would like to point out that what is being called an OD intervention is also an event based on behavioral science theory and application and may be called something other than an OD technique. Let us address the last question first. The conditions necessary to support an OD intervention are a problem, vaguely or clearly perceived by management; a willingness to address the problem; and, most important, support from top management, who are willing to provide resources to resolve the problem. The criteria for selecting an OD intervention are that it responds to an actual or felt need by the client, involves the client in planning and implementing the change (two of Burke's criteria, 1994), provides valid and useful information relevant to the problem, and is chosen by the client, who feels responsible for implementing it (internal commitment). The last three items are from Argyris (1970). Because we are describing an OD intervention rather than an OD program, we have not included Burke's third criterion, a change in the organizational culture. Below are some guidelines to consider in designing an intervention. In some cases the intervenors may be a consulting team, an individual consultant, or a manager within the system. The guidelines can be applicable to all three intervenors. Some interventions, such as an initial interview, spontaneous process comments, or sending a client to a workshop, may not entail all these guidelines. They can also be thought of as "what consultants typically do" to help the manager formulate his or her own program.

1. A consultant's presence in the client system *is* an intervention. We have discussed this item above.

2. It is important to be certain that as complete a job as possible has been done in diagnosing the problem situation. This step may include interviewing key personnel and using diagnostic instruments and questionnaires to obtain information from the employees involved. It may be tempting to use commercial instruments because they appear more scientific, even though they may not be the best fit to defining the problem. Designing your own diagnostic instrument with scales or questions you want to ask may be more relevant to clarifying the problem area. The data collected can then be subjected to a "scientific" analysis through the use of statistical procedures if this is appropriate.

3. Once the data have been collated and organized, one must identify, in specific and concrete form, the issues or problems to be addressed. It is important that the design team is in agreement that these *are* problems.

4. It is important not to jump to or suggest interventions until the team has completed the diagnosis and defined the problems to be addressed. It may be very tempting to do this, that is, provide a solution before you understand the nature of the problem.

5. It is important for the team to be clear on what they are designing for and why it would work. It is also important to consider a theoretical basis for interventions rather than to dump techniques on a client system because the consultant "likes" them.

6. The intervention or design should be tested on a colleague or members of the client system.
- Are the instructions clear?
- Is the flow logical stepwise?
- How would you react if you were a participant in the intervention?
- Is it likely that your intervention will meet your diagnosed goal(s)?
- How will you know if the intervention is successful?

7. The goals of the intervention must be sufficiently clear, objective, and concrete to measure the degree to which the intervention was successful. The plans for the intervention should include the retrieval of data and a design for processing the data, whether the intervention succeeds or fails. Sometimes a failed intervention provides more learning for participants than a successful one. In addition, sloppy or incomplete data retrieval leads to highly questionable diagnoses or problem identification.

8. For smooth execution, it should be decided very clearly who is going to do what before, during, and after the intervention. This role assignment will help to avoid duplication or gaps in the execution of the intervention.

9. All intervenors should take complete responsibility for the entire sequence of events: initiating, implementing, closing, and evaluating. Whether or not a role is assigned, each individual should be ready to step in and take responsibility at any stage of the intervention. This step will avoid problems due to absenteeism or late arrival of any of the intervenors.

10. After all the preparations are completed, it is very useful to "walk through" the total intervention to make certain everyone and everything is clearly understood. At this point, inconsistencies and discrepancies may be spotted. This procedure prior to the execution of the intervention leaves time for last-minute changes.

11. A word of caution. Sometimes everyone agrees with everyone else because each person believes it is what everyone else wants, even though he or she may not want it individually. This dilemma is known as the "Abilene Paradox" (Harvey, 1988). The family agreed to take a ride to Abilene only because each member thought that was the desire of every other member. Once the dilemma was discussed, they discovered that no one really wanted to go to Abilene. The same paradox can arise when there is a group of intervenors making decisions about designing and implementation. The consultant team members need to be up front with their feelings and opinions about what is going on, particularly when they are in the minority.

Is strategic planning (SP) an
OD intervention? Should it be?

An answer could be "yes and no." If an OD consultant suggests SP to the client, then SP is an OD intervention. If there is no OD consultant or program involved, then SP is not an OD intervention. This is not to say that OD technology is necessarily absent. There are many SP experts (who are not OD consultants) who help organizations to do SP. OD consultants, however, can help an organization to set up, design, and work through the various steps in SP. The setting up, designing, and working through is an important learning process itself, and how these activities are done is as important as the content of the activities themselves.

French and Bell (1990) defined *strategic management* (of which SP is an integral activity) as "development and implementation of the organization's 'grand design' or overall strategy in relation to its current and future environmental demands" (p. 166). At least two major factors are involved in the OD/SP development. Previously, most OD was focused internally and involved itself with team building, problem solving, intergroup relations, role clarification, conflict resolution, and so forth. In the past decade, there has been a shift away from immediate internal problems to external environments with which the organization is involved, and from dealing with immediate (present) problems to planning for the future. The paradigm might look like this:

Internal status → current external environments
Present status → possible future environments

In the following SP outline, the integration of OD technology will become more obvious. The outline consists of elements from Beckhard and Harris (1977), Schendel and Hofer (1979), Summer (1980, Chap. 10), Rogers (1981, cited in French & Bell, 1990, p. 167), Krone (1974, cited in French & Bell, 1990, pp. 167, 168), and Jayaram (1976).

In preparation for the SP meetings, the executives and managers familiarize themselves with the financial status of the organization, its competition, and its immediate socioenvironmental situation. They may also prepare, individually, a statement of how they see the organization's mission. The stress here is on how they see the organization as a whole, not their own departments.

A critical part of the first SP meeting is to produce a mission statement. The individual perceptions can be collated until a statement is arrived at to everyone's satisfaction. Another strategy to arrive at a mission statement is to ask, "What business are we in?" Mission statements form the basis of the SP activities. A clear mission statement enables managers to identify more clearly how their own departments contribute to the overall goals of the organization. They can then develop their own departmental mission statements more relevant to the organization's mission.

Organizations do not exist independent of their environments but are in an ongoing interactive condition in which they affect and are affected by various entities. Once a clear and comprehensive mission statement is developed, a next step is to identify and analyze the current demands made upon the organization by the external environment. Rogers (1981, cited in French & Bell, 1990, p. 167) called these environments "domains" and identified four of them: suppliers, customers, competitors, and regulators. Albrecht (1983) subdivided the overall environments even further: customer, competitor, economic, social, technological, political, legal, and physical. The current environmental analysis includes the external opportunities and threats that exist to the organization. What is the organization doing to take advantage of the opportunities, and what is it doing to guard against, adapt to, or resolve the threats? What are the organization's responses to these current demands? At this point, the organization needs to look inward to identify and analyze its own strengths and weaknesses in responding to the external threats and opportunities. The focus here is on the organization's own operations, resources, allocation of responsibilities, and marketing activities. This inward look represents a comprehensive assessment of the organization as an adaptive entity that uncovers disparities between what is and what ought to be. It examines "the quality of the 'environmental match'—the extent to which the enterprise is attuned to the major flow of events in the environment which will affect its health and survival" (Albrecht, 1983, p. 189). After analyzing the present scenario, strategic planners look ahead and predict realistic future scenarios. What would happen if the organization made no adaptive changes in response to possible future environmental changes?

This process highlights the adequacy or inadequacy of current organizational responses. This information can then be used to revamp current responses to meet future demands. A desired state of affairs or ideal situation between the projected future demands and the projected organization's responses can be envisioned. Blake and Mouton's (1968) *ideal strategic corporate model* provides a goal toward (and away from) which movement can be measured. In the design of a present and future analysis of internal and external variables, a TOWS matrix (Weihrich, 1982) may prove useful.

	Internal Strengths (S)	Internal Weaknesses (W)
External Opportunities (O)	SO	WO
External Threats (T)	ST	WT

Figure 5.1. TOWS Matrix
SOURCE: Weihrich, 1982, p. 60.

The external environmental factors are the opportunities (O) and threats (T); the internal factors include the organizations strengths (S) and weaknesses (W). The matrix can be used to look at the current situation. It can then be projected into the future. The strategy is then to maximize the external opportunities and internal strengths and to reduce the external threats and internal weaknesses (see Figure 5.1).

The strategy of the matrix is to create planning statements that combine internal strengths and weaknesses with external opportunities and threats (i.e., SO, WO, ST, WT). These planning statements are strategies for addressing optimal relationships between internal and external environmental factors. They describe specific actions to be implemented.

The last phase of the SP is to examine the feasibility, cost effectiveness, and consequences (intended and unintended) of the action plans. This component involves creating a monitoring system to track the objectives, developing criteria by which to measure the extent of goal achievement, agreeing upon target dates for completion of objectives and instituting follow-up reviews and evaluations.

Each phase of SP involves group activities such as full and open participation of all members, exploration of all alternatives and options, productive management of disagreements, a consensus model for decision making, monitoring of individual-oriented agendas (i.e., agendas of those who are entrenched in their own disciplines or departments), and creating a climate of openness, risk taking, and concern for individual and organizational needs. SP requires successful facilitation of group process. OD consultants can fulfill this role. They can also help managers assess their current strategies, assess the process by which these strategies are developed, and get a more effective strategy-planning process established. OD and SP should be complementary rather than competitive. There is a need for OD theorists and practitioners to expand and improve their contributions to SP. "We believe organization development practitioners need to become experts in strategic management *process* and need to have more than just a cursory knowledge of strategic management *content*" (French & Bell, 1990, p. 168).

What are some examples of an OD intervention?

Below are two examples of an intervention. The first is a short excerpt of what would be a lengthier initial interview between a consultant and a client.

Consultant: Can you give me some idea of the kinds of issues or problems you'd like to address?

Client: Well, we have a communication problem.

Consultant: OK, that's a little broad. Can you be more specific? Give me a "for instance."

Client: I get together with my managers once every 2 weeks, and we set short-term objectives for their first-line supervisors. Two weeks later, we end up missing our deadlines.

Consultant: Where do you see the communication break down?

Client: Between the managers and the first-line supervisors.

Consultant: You see the late deadlines to be a consequence of a communication breakdown between your managers and their first-line supervisors? Let's hold the late deadlines for a moment. I'd like to get more of your ideas on that later. When you get together with your managers, how do you work out the objectives?

Client: I tell them what's needed.

Consultant: Do you do anything else to make sure they all heard you right?

Client: What do you mean?

Consultant: Well, like putting the objectives in writing and checking to make sure everyone understands them in the same way, or having them summarize their understanding of what you said?

Client: No, I didn't see any need to. I don't have any problem saying what I mean.

Consultant: Do you think it is possible that they have trouble picking up what you mean from what you say?

Client: I don't know. That's a thought. I assumed that because they never asked questions, they understood what I said. How can we check that out?

Three possible problem areas emerge from this interview: (a) the nature of the communication breakdown (if any) between the managers and the first-line supervisors; (b) one-way communication between the client and the managers (i.e., client tells them what is needed; does the client solicit from the managers their ideas of what is needed?) (c) one-way communication again; the client does not check for understanding of what he or she communicated. The consultant begins as a facilitator by focusing on what the client thinks is the problem. The last response of the client indicates that he or she is beginning to get some insight into a possible communication problem between him- or herself and the managers.

The second intervention represented a massive effort to change the culture in the receiving clinics of 176 Veteran Affairs hospitals and outpatient clinics. This intervention was part of a larger program to revamp the ambulatory system agency-wide. The Receiving Unit is the first point of contact concerning delivery of medical care. Experiences and impressions gained here by the veteran shape his or her evaluation of all the medical treatment received and may influence his or her rehabilitation. Unfortunately, many complaints regarding ineffective and discourteous handling of veterans seeking medical treatment have been voiced throughout the VA hospital system. The Receiving Clinics became hotbeds of dissatisfaction and tension fueled by long hours of waiting and lack of personal attention for veterans and their families. This atmosphere was managed by low-level clerks (GS 2 and 3) who were themselves victims of burnout from long hours on the "firing lines." Part of the reorganization of the Receiving Clinics included a systematic training program for personnel who had initial contact with the incoming veterans. Shortly after its initiation, the training program (Training for Individual and Group Effectiveness and Resourcefulness, TIGER; Hanson & Peck, 1974) was incorporated to include all VA personnel. The program was designed to increase awareness of and sensitivity to the process of interpersonal communication, elements that constitute the helping relationship, conflict management, team building, and effective utilization of team resources in problem solving. The program consisted of three phases:

1. *Twelve experimental hospitals*—Training of trainers for the 12 hospitals who were to institute a training program in their own hospital. This training consisted of 2 weeks of workshops and a 2-day follow-up. To provide administrative support for the training, 35 participants consisting of chiefs of Medicine and Medical Administration Services and allied personnel from the Central Office participated in a 1-week workshop on developing organizational effectiveness.

2. *VA hospital system-wide training*—This phase consisted of five 1-week intensive training-of-trainers workshops located strategically at different facilities throughout the country. These workshops involved some 250 participants and were held in Houston, San Francisco, Boston, Atlanta, and Chicago.

3. *District resource trainers*—Phase 3 involved the selection of 55 trainers from the five basic workshops to become district consultant/trainers. The selection of these individuals was based upon peer and staff evaluations. These trainers received an additional 2 weeks of advanced training. As consultants, they were to provide consultation and backup support for the trainers within their districts. Handbooks were developed for all hospitals (Hanson, 1973; Hanson et al., 1977). From the inception of the program in 1972 to its completion in 1978, some 400 to 500 trainers, 56 district consultants, and more than 35,000 participants were involved. To date, this program was probably the most extensive application of behavioral science theories and techniques in an organization as large as the Veterans Affairs hospital system.

Does this program qualify as OD? According to Burke's criteria (1994), it does. First, if we think of the VA system as the client, the TIGER program responded to an actual and perceived need—complaints system-wide from veterans and their families. In addition, the program involved the client(s) in the planning and implementation of the effort. It was an employees' program conducted by employees from all services and from all levels within hospitals. Meetings were held with Central Office personnel concerning program issues and progress, and 500 VA personnel were selected for training by hospital administrators to design their own programs, with help from the Houston staff, to fit their own hospitals' needs (which included data collection from their own personnel). Finally, the culture of the hospitals, particularly the Receiving Units, was influenced significantly in many hospitals where the TIGER program was fully accepted and in force. Ombudspersons were created and placed in Receiving Units to respond to veterans' and their families' questions and needs; support workshops were instituted for "front-line" receiving clerks; there was an atmosphere of "community" among staff and personnel; and TIGER and related programs (e.g., team building, supervisory leadership workshops, consultation skills, communication, stress management) continued for 2 years after termination of Central Office funding.

In the front-end contracting process, how do you position an OD intervention to increase the probability of success?

We can assume that the client system feels the need for some consultation on a organizational or subsystem problem. The problem may be clear, as in the case of low productivity, low morale, or ineffective decision making, or vague, as in the case of "things not going well" or a sense that things could be better. In any event, it is important for the success of the intervention that key people, especially top management, recognize the problem and be willing to give support and be involved. It is also important to receive support from the surrounding same and higher work unit levels. Because the OD consultant's methods are primarily based on the behavioral sciences, recognition of the applicability of this methodology to the problem by a higher level influential person is highly desirable. If the consultant cannot get all of the active support he or she would like, he or she may have to settle for a willingness to wait and see. It is to be hoped that this willingness will include an intention not to hinder or sabotage the intervention. If these conditions are met, the consultant has to consider what he or she needs to do and facilitate in order to increase the potential for an effective intervention. The following criteria for an effective intervention are summarized from Argyris (1970).

The consultant must collect *valid* and *useful* information that accurately reflects what members perceive and feel are their primary concerns and issues and what they would like to see changed. This is similar to Burke's (1994) "actual and felt need for change." If the information reflects the needs of the members, then it is valid. If it suggests or indicates directions for change, then it is useful.

Free choice indicates that the locus of decision making is in the client system. No prescribed action is imposed on the client. The client is given a blueprint of the situation (diagnosis) and alternatives for action. It is the client who determines the course of action related to the central needs of the organization's members. This action is based on an accurate analysis and not on biases of a subgroup or the defenses of the decision makers.

Internal commitment means that the client owns the choice and feels responsible for its implementation. It is important, therefore, that the client is involved in diagnosing, planning, and implementing the intervention. The members act on their choice because it responds to their individual and organizational needs. There is very little dependence on others for action.

It is probably obvious throughout these responses to questions that many of the guidelines for developing OD programs or interventions, whether for subsystems or for the total organization, repeat themselves. Much of this similarity is due to an underlying OD philosophy and theory that is internally relatively consistent.

Can an OD intervention succeed without a reorientation of the personal perspectives of the client's management teams?

It is not likely. Much may depend upon the team's prior management philosophy and orientation. If the leadership style of the team has been such that the team leader makes most of the decisions with or without the team members' participation, then an OD intervention will entail a reorientation. Under an authoritarian philosophy, team members may make suggestions and comments about an issue to be resolved, but are not empowered to participate in the actual decision making concerning a course of action or its actual resolution. The team leader may or may not use the information provided by the team members in making his or her decision. This style of team management fosters dependency and a lack of initiative and sense of power among team members. These conditions are antithetical to OD philosophy, which seeks to empower team members by enabling them to participate in the decisions that affect their work life. This latter kind of participation fosters a sense of ownership and responsibility to implement the decisions and to work with the consequences.

If the management style of the team already contains many of the elements consistent with OD assumptions, then a reorientation may be minimal or not needed at all. The OD intervention may simply add value and competence to what is already present in the team's mode of operations.

Can an OD intervention succeed and exclude cultural transformation in an organization?

It is not clear what the questioner means by *culture*. There are two pos-sibilities: One is *organizational culture* as defined in Chapter 1, and the other is the cultural makeup of the members of the organization (e.g., race, ethnicity, and gender). In either case, the answer is *no*. In the first case, one of Burke's (1994) criteria for an OD program is that it leads to changes in the organization's culture (e.g., from managers' self-authorized decisions to organization members' participation in decision making, or from man-agers' fixing blame for a problem and attempting to solve it themselves to managers' working with team members to address the problem). Vaill (1989a) wondered "why we keep talking as if there were not cultural forces invisibly influencing *all* thought and action in an organization" (p. 13). The OD interventionist must diagnose the organization's culture and share this information with the client to determine what issues or problems can or cannot be addressed at that time. Some cultural elements may be so ingrained that to address them directly and immediately would be met with strong resistance and subsequent failure. Success of initial interventions may loosen up the more ingrained organizational norms so that they may be more accessible to later interventions.

The second case refers to the multicultural makeup of the workforce. More than 12% of the American workforce is black, with Hispanics closing fast and Asians moving up behind. Almost half the workforce consists of women. Yet white males outnumber all other segments in the population in supervisory, management, and professional jobs in proportion to their numbers in the general population (Albrecht, 1983). When we consider that American companies are increasingly involved in business relations with foreign countries, the multicultural aspect of our own organizations will be and is a major concern of OD. Other countries, particularly in the Third World, may look at the racial, ethnic, and sexual makeup of our organizations, particularly at the higher levels, and ask, "Do we practice what we preach?"

What is the relevance of OD to a "management-of-diversity" intervention?

Any major changes or cultural shifts in the constituency of the workforce that affect organizations will be grist for the mill for OD practitioners' philosophy and methodology. Efforts must be made toward creating a workplace where diversity is valued, where the reward system is based on competence regardless of sex, race, ethnicity, age, alternate lifestyle, and physical ability/disability, and where cultural, group, and individual differences are appreciated. We cannot ignore the descriptions of the workforce predicted for the year 2000:

> Women, people of color, and immigrants (many non-English speaking) represent more than 50 percent of the present workforce.
>
> By 2000, 85% of the entering workforce will be female, African-American, Asian-American, Latino, or new immigrants.
>
> Two million "older" workers, between ages 50 and 64, are ready, willing, and able to work and are not being utilized. Within twenty-five years, one out of every four workers will be age 55 or older.
>
> Of the 43 million people with disabilities in this country, many will seek equal opportunity in employment, encouraged by the Americans with Disabilities Act of 1990. (Blank & Slipp, 1994, p. 3)

In this multicultural setting there will be different expectations in work styles, needs, and values. Managers need to be (or become) sensitive to these differences as well as looking inward toward their own values and how these values are reflected in their day-to-day behavior. OD consultants also need to be aware of their own values in this regard if they are going to be useful to clients in addressing issues and problems involving diversity.

This soul-searching needs to begin with the individuals themselves who are going to facilitate the exploration of clients' expectations, attitudes, beliefs, and feelings. The process can then turn outward to look at the extent to which these factors are embedded in their own departments and in the organization's policies, operations, and philosophy. Awareness of others is always best when it is preceded by self-awareness.

In Chapters 3, we stressed the importance of consultants' examining their own values. We may not be aware of many of our values and how they affect our relationships with others. We may espouse some values verbally but behave in a way that does not reflect these values. Unfortunately, we may not be aware of this discrepancy. Many of our biases are based on values (e.g., a bias toward participative group decision making is a reflection of a value). Biases, however, also may represent negative values that we may disown or deny, but that are present anyway and influence our behavior. When we deny or disown aspects of ourselves, we lose control of our behavior and act out those aspects unwittingly. In a group or team setting where the exploration of these types of issues is legitimate, an OD consultant, with his or her behavioral science background, can facilitate this process.

Related to biases and values are stereotypes. Most books on diversity will address the problem of stereotyping. Stereotypes are images we hold about a category of people or things. These images are held by a large number of people. Stereotypes are shorthand ways of classifying people. They can be positive or negative (e.g., police, blacks, whites, artists, old, young, male, female). When our impressions of people are governed by stereotypes, we infer things about them from their social category and ignore things that are inconsistent with our stereotype. That is, we engage in a process of selective attention, attending to behaviors that support our stereotype and not attending to discrepant behaviors. Unfortunately, negatively stereotyped individuals or groups are at a disadvantage. Once they are stereotyped, it is assumed that certain behaviors are present in them, or potentially present, even if these behaviors have never manifested themselves. Stereotypes, once established, are resistant to change. Most are based on untested assumptions that, in turn, keep them alive. We treat our untested assumptions as if they were the truth or fact, not needing to be examined. Furthermore, we act on them as if they were true, doing the stereotyped individual a great disservice. They then become the basis for self-fulfilling prophecies. The power of stereotypes and their resistance to change may lie in the degree of emotional investment we have in them. Again, these behaviors can be explored with clients, along with the extent to which they influence decisions the manager makes (e.g., "Let's put him behind a desk at the rear of the office so customers won't see his wheelchair"; "Women are too emotional to handle this job, it requires a strong rational approach").

The use of stereotypes is one of two offenses that Blank and Slipp (1994) identified as workplace problems. The other occurs when managers or others ignore a group characteristic or tendency that may influence one's behavior and perspective. On the one hand, each person is innately different from other individuals: "We are not all the same" (p. 6). On the other hand, people do have some common characteristics or experiences that may influence or enhance their work behavior. These common characteristics constitute their group identity. "When group identity is recognized, it is often in terms of stereotypes—categorizing individuals *only* by their group identity—rather than seeing the group identity as one part of a complex individual. Such stereotyping is often characterized by blatantly negative or mistaken interpretations of a group tendency" (p. 7).

Miller, in a preface to *The Promise of Diversity* (Cross, Katz, Miller, & Seashore, 1994), identified two approaches to diversity: the individual differences perspective and the social justice perspective. The first approach focuses on what has already been accomplished and strives to create understanding between and among different individuals. The second addresses the inequities and oppressions that exist in organizations (institutional "isms").

> To achieve the promise of diversity we need to hear, understand and appreciate the voice of Individual Differences *and* the voice of Social Justice. We need to recognize that both voices are not only valid but necessary. *Both* must be heard and acted upon to bring about an inclusive organizational culture. (p. xxix)

The task for OD consultants is how to get clients to address these issues effectively in their own organizations, even when the client contracts for this type of intervention; that is, how to create an atmosphere of mutual respect, listening, and understanding in which significant dialogue can take place. Working with diversity is risky, in part because individuals are being asked to address issues they have long kept under wraps and in part because they may have disowned their own prejudices and do not want their self-image of being nonjudgmental threatened.

Blank and Slipp (1994) offered some guidelines for the manager or supervisor, a few of which will be summarized here (pp. 192-193):

- Approach every employee as an individual—do not make assumptions on the basis of group identity.
- Understand that cultural tendencies such as language, mannerisms, and communication patterns are not necessarily indicators of a worker's performance and capabilities.
- Recognize and confront the issue of discomfort—your own and others'—in dealing with a diverse workforce.
- Use equal performance standards for all workers.
- Provide feedback often and equally to all members of the workforce.
- Openly support the competencies and contribution of workers from all groups.
- Be aware of subtle and systemic institutional discrimination, intentional or unintentional, that pigeonholes and limits opportunities for members of groups other than those in the dominant culture.
- Confront racist, sexist, or other stereotypic or discriminatory behavior.
- Become comfortable asking questions about preferred terminology or interactions.
- Finally, understand that you, the manager, ultimately hold the key for releasing the full potential of each person in your work unit.

A major goal for organizations is "to make valuing diversity a bedrock value" (Cobbs, 1994, p. 27). We have frequently read or heard about a person's *core values*, or fundamental values that guide the way an individual lives his or her life. Core values are difficult to change and are resistant to others' attempts to change them. Organizations also have core values that support their philosophy and guide their behavior. Cobbs (1994) believes that "only when valuing diversity as a core value of our organizations will we begin to be uncomfortable when we do not see diversity" (p. 27). This statement reflects the critical mass theory. Once a critical mass is reached, those behaviors not representative of this mass are seen as deviant and receive no support for their continuance.

Should those accountable for change in an organization have any understanding of the OD process?

It depends upon the sophistication of the client, if that is what the party meant by "those accountable for change." If the accountable person is the client's superior, the response below is applicable to him or her as well. The client may be more intimately involved than his or her superior, and may obtain his or her understanding experientially as well as intellectually. The client's superior may not be involved in the intervention and may require only an intellectual understanding. We will respond at the client level.

In some cases the client is fairly knowledgeable about the process; this is why the client hired an OD practitioner in the first place. A client who has some understanding of the process makes the consultant's job easier. A client who has little or no understanding of the process has to be educated by the consultant. How this education is obtained depends upon the client's willingness to be educated and upon the resources available. One way is to have the client attend workshops. Another way is for the consultant to work with the client, involving him or her in a step-by-step progression of the intervention. This involves sharing perceptions, feelings, understanding, and rationales of what is happening and what may be expected to happen. If part of the consultant's job is to facilitate the client's skill development and theoretical understanding of the OD process, it should begin here. A client who understands the process is much more likely to support the intervention and to assume responsibility for it. A consultant who does not involve the client in the educational process of an OD intervention is violating one of the basic principles of OD philosophy.

What kind of costs are we talking about? Do we need tools? Can a small firm afford an OD intervention?

The cost of an OD program or an OD intervention varies considerably. Two major factors need to be taken into consideration: the OD consultant and the scope of the program (e.g., team building vs. total organization). The cost of instruments (tools) such as surveys, rating scales, questionnaires, whether commercial or self-developed, is minimal. The time and effort spent in organizing and interpreting data from these instruments may be charged separately or included in the consultant's daily rate.

OD consultants' fees typically may range from $500 to $3,500 a day, depending upon the expertise and reputation of the consultant and what the organization can afford and is willing to pay. These fees do not include expenses. Some consultants may go as high as $10,000 a day for interventions and programs that are specific to certain current issues (e.g., diversity) and are in demand by the organization. OD consultants may also vary their own fees depending upon what the organization can afford and the interests of the consultants themselves. Many times the fee is negotiated between the consultant and the client. The fee is also influenced by competition, how badly a consultant wants the contract, and how busy a consultant is with other clients.

The scope of the program and the size of the organization will also influence the cost. A full OD program that involves the total organization and entails several years will, of course, be more costly than an intervention in a subunit of the company. For example, a team-building effort in one department of a large organization or with the top management of a small company is going to be smaller in scope and cost less than a total organizational effort. This total effort will involve greater breadth in the inclusion of subsystems and greater depth in the layers of management responsibilities and authority. Like any other enterprise, it is important to shop around for a "best fit" between the client's needs and what the consultant has to offer to meet these needs. This is true for small firms as well as large organizations.

OD Compared to Other Change Technologies

How do terms like _organizational transformation_ (_OT_), _organizational behavior_ (_OB_), and _organizational effectiveness_ (_OE_) relate to OD?

These terms are not mutually exclusive of OD; in fact, they are largely synonymous with it. OT uses methodologies that could easily be described as participative OD approaches. In OT change efforts, however, there is a strong orientation toward the future and a massive attempt at changing the culture and direction of the organization (French & Bell, 1990). Weisbord (1987) described OT as a "discontinuous rapid culture change helped by novel questions about myths, heroes, rituals, unwritten rules, values, etc." (p. 256). Both OD and OT interchange their perspectives and techniques. Both the above definitions include large and quick cultural changes in the organization. Although the terms differ, the important thing is to identify and understand the underlying processes. This brings us to the Webster's (1988) definition of _transformation,_ which highlights the "process of changing from an abstract underlying structure into a surface structure." This change is brought about by the utilization of certain orderly and systematic rules. In OT this process would involve surfacing such underlying, abstract cultural structures as norms, unspoken values, cherished rituals, the organization's heroes, and myths that are held up as models. Once these structures and their influence are explicit or "visible," they can be addressed in terms of their value to the direction in which the organization wants to go. Again, much of this process is common to both OD and OT.

OB appears to overlap with OD even more. It stems from and supersedes the earlier term *human relations.* "OB concerns the improvement of effectiveness of the human organization (people systems) of industrial, governmental and other institutions. It emphasizes a systems approach" (Lau, 1975, p. 8). OB deals with four levels of behavior and their effectiveness: the individual, the work group and team, intergroup coordination, and the total organization. To develop these four levels, OB utilizes knowledge, skills, and perspectives from behavioral sciences (which Lau calls *social technology*), from Theory Y leadership philosophy, and from the leader as a facilitator and change agent.

How does OB differ from OD? One consultant's comment was, "OB is the academic framework; OD has theories." One superficial difference is that OB uses the term *behavior* to emphasize that an organization is made up of people in many types of relationships, and that the effectiveness of their behavior is the focus. The "development" part of the OD term focuses on the behavior of people in the organization and the processes involved in their interactions and relationships. The difference between the two is more academic than real.

Organizational effectiveness (OE) is a term we encountered when doing an OD project for the army chaplain service. During the latter phase of this program, we discovered that the "line" officers had developed an OE program for the army's line personnel (the OE Center at Fort Ord, California, graduated 1,702 officers as internal consultants). The theories and methodologies that the OE program utilized were the same as those of our OD project. The differences in terms may not reflect a difference in substance. The term OE describes an outcome that may involve various functions of an organizational improvement program. Unlike OD, it is not a program that has its own theory or set of methodologies. OE is a construct that may include any number of measures to evaluate progress in a variety of organizational processes. In a review of the literature, Campbell (1977, cited in Chisholm, 1983, p. 12) found over 30 criteria that might have been used to determine OE (e.g., productivity, efficiency, quality, and control). Other measures included job satisfaction, motivation, absenteeism and turnover, and flexibility/adaptation. Campbell further stated that the construct is so complex that the potential exists for measures to conflict with one another. In some descriptions, OE appears to be an outcome of OD programs.

What is organizational learning?

You can teach someone to solve a problem, but the person may not become a better problem solver. What the individual may not have learned was a *process* for solving problems. We are reminded of an old adage, "Give a person a fish, and feed him for a day. Teach him to fish, and he can feed himself for a lifetime." A consultant can help organization members to correct problems, but that does not necessarily mean that they learn a different way of solving problems. For organizations to develop their own learning process, members need to involve themselves in systems thinking (see Chapter 4). Managers must not only see the organization as a whole, but be aware of how subsystems relate to each other and affect the overall pattern (Senge, 1990). Again, we emphasize the importance of *process* learning (see Chapter 1): how decisions are made and problems solved, how subsystems work together and affect organizational goals, and how the organizational culture facilitates or inhibits effective problem solving and work relationships.

On an individual basis, the concept of "learning how to learn," noted above, has relevance to group and organizational levels. Learning how to learn is a process through which continued personal and professional growth is possible. This process is accomplished by (a) a willingness to examine one's values and how they affect one's choices; (b) the assumption of an experimental attitude toward one's own behavior and toward one's problems in living; (c) a willingness to take risks, particularly when the risk involves the potential for greater learning; and (d) the creation of a climate for oneself and others in which learning will be a continuous process (Hanson, 1981, pp. 8-9).

Does the term *learning organization* include OD methodology?

The concept of the learning organization emphasizes the learning process itself and the idea that it involves everyone in the organization at all levels. Everyone is primarily a learner in a never-ending process of learning and improvement. Senge (1990) described a learning organization as a place "where people continually expand their capacity to create the results they truly desire, where new and expansive patterns of thinking are nurtured, where collective aspiration is set free, and where people are continually learning how to learn together" (p. 3). People learn from their accomplishments as well as from their mistakes. The experience of learning, whether from success or failure, is passed on to others so that they may use this information to produce their own continuous learning and improvement. The organization provides a vision and a direction geared to utilize and promote every person's creativity to the fullest in order to generate the best outcomes. It is important that "results are secondary to the process and [to the] breakthroughs that lead to success" (Lader, 1988, p. 35, cited in Schmidt & Finnegan, 1993, p. 136). This point has been noted in several of the questions and responses: Solving a problem is important, but learning the process of problem solving (i.e., how to solve problems) is more important.

Some of the features of learning organizations are that people have the freedom to think for themselves, to be proactive, and to make decisions; there is a high level of involvement of all members; feedback is used for learning and clarifying what needs to be changed; members who have the most resources for a particular problem are utilized to the fullest; there is an emphasis on clear, direct, and accurate communication at all levels; and mistakes are not punished but are used as a source for continuous learning and improvement. These elements of a learning organization are common to other systems, particularly TQM and TQI, as well as to OD. The emphasis on process, building effective learning teams, using feedback as part of the learning process, establishing clear and open communications, and creating a climate in which individuals' creativity and opportunity to contribute are enhanced certainly reflects OD goals and methodology.

Does the concept of sociotechnical systems (STS) include OD?

Some years ago, organizations were thought to be technical systems operating in a rational framework for the production and distribution of their resources. Later, through the expanding influence of the behavioral sciences, people were increasingly being seen as an integral component of the organization, and it was realized that in addition to job functions, workers' activities and relationships had a critical impact on the technical system. The human element was referred to as the *social system*. Both systems are intimately enmeshed, and it is difficult and risky to consider one without the other.

The concept of STS was developed from studies at the Tavistock Institute in England, mainly by Trist, in the 1940s and early 1950s (Trist, 1982). STS seeks "to develop a better fit between the technology structures and social interaction of the work place so as to achieve desired organizational and human objectives" (Shani & Elliott, 1989, p. 188). This better fit can be achieved in work units in a mine, a factory, an office, the public or the private sector, and union or nonunion organizations. "By examining the fit or lack of fit between the needs of the people and the nature of the work they do, solutions are found to problems concerning quality, productivity, absenteeism, turnover, costs and adaptability to change" (Pasmore & Sherwood, 1994).

In STS, there is a strong emphasis on semiautonomous work groups and on working with management and unions. The theory emphasizes "the need to design jobs that give employees control over the key variances of an organization's production or services. This has typically been accomplished by forming self directing autonomous work groups that have major responsibility for task performance" (Pasmore & Sherwood, 1978, p. 4). STS also involves quality of work life theory in that it emphasizes uniting union and management to create greater job security and creating high-quality products, services, and relationships across functions and levels and between customers and producers (Weisbord, 1987). STS is currently addressing such organizational issues as the introduction of new technology requirements for improving working life, increasing workforce flexibility, increasing quality, and reducing costs (Cotter & Mohr, 1984). STS and OD share theories and technologies and appear to be moving closer to each other. Such items as increasing skills and responsibilities of lower echelon employees, creating more of a partnership between manager and employee, designing new structures requiring perceptual, communication, and leadership skills, and espousing an open-systems philosophy that is sensitive and responsive to the environment and to differences in other organizations are common to both OD and STS.

Quality circles (QC) or quality control circles—is this OD?

Quality circles were used extensively in Japan since the introduction of quality control techniques by Deming (1986) and Juran (1988, 1989) in the 1950s and 1960s. A quality circle usually consists of 7 to 10 employees, either within similar work units or across units. They meet regularly on a voluntary basis to identify problems, analyze their causes, make recommendations to management, and, with management's approval, implement solutions. The circles are usually chaired by a supervisor but can be chaired by an employee selected by the group. Before the circles begin to function, the prospective leaders are trained by quality control experts or facilitators trained in QC concepts. This training includes the use of statistical tools, practice in leading participative group discussion, group dynamics, and communication skills.

These circles link up with other groups or circles to coordinate activities, use expert resources when needed, make changes without requiring higher authority when feasible, and meet with higher management several times a year. They are primarily self-directed and given a considerable amount of responsibility.

Several assumptions underlie QC. First, employees are willing to collaborate with their superiors in a team setting. Second, employees can learn to use both technical and process consultants effectively. Third, employees have considerable capability and potentially high-quality insights into work life, provided they are trained in QC concepts and tools (i.e., measuring techniques, group dynamics, team leadership, and interpersonal communication). Fourth, the heterogeneity of the groups provides a variety of perspectives. Some of the consequences of these programs are improved relationships among employees, an increase in employee motivation, increased identification with the company, decrease in costs, and a movement toward participative management (Huczynski, 1987, p. 241).

From the above description, the congruence with OD is obvious: attention to group dynamics, participative group meetings with supervisors, use of facilitators, participative diagnosis and problem solving, addressing of intergroup issues, and multifunctional teams working on mutually identified problems. OD does not, however, focus only on quality control matters. One danger in QC is that some companies become more mechanistic, focusing primarily on statistical techniques, quality, and a "by-the-book approach," with little attention to the more human interactive aspects cited above.

How does OD relate to quality of work life (QWL)?

There is no clear-cut definition of QWL. There is a wide variety of perspectives on what characterizes a high-quality work situation. Different segments of the workforce have different interpretations of what quality of work life means to them (Levine, Taylor, & Davis, 1984). The movement, if *movement* is an appropriate term, represents a response to a shift in values and attitudes among young employees toward work. Another factor has been the increasing pressure on organizations to be more productive and more responsive to citizen and client needs (Chisholm, 1983). QWL philosophy views the employees as a key organizational resource. Given the right conditions, employees will contribute to improving the quality of their work experience and, at the same time, improve the overall effectiveness of the organization. They will also make meaningful contributions to the goals of the organization.

QWL represents a "commitment by a company to work improvement and to the creation of more satisfying and attractive jobs and working environments for all its employees" (Huczynski, 1987, p. 244). QWL attempts to link the individual's developmental needs to the goals and growth of the organization. Some of the basic characteristics are unions and management working together to plan changes and the redesigning of jobs, a commitment to work in groups or teams assuming responsibility for their own supervision and quality control, and a focus on recognizing and addressing the sociotechnical nature of the organization. QWL may also include quality circles.

It is apparent that QWL, QC, and, as described below, total quality management (TQM) and total quality improvement (TQI) have much in common. What makes them related to OD are some basic common features: union involvement, a focus on work teams, problem-solving sessions by work teams, some autonomy in planning work, availability of skill training, and closer working relationships between employees and management. OD does not decide which job structure is best, what are the most effective safety guidelines, or what requirements are needed for increased production. It does provide, however, a process by which these issues can be addressed. Chisholm (1983) stated that the

> adoption of a perspective which recognizes the systemic nature of changes required to support and foster QWL attempts is essential. The planned change (OD) approach tends to build in this point of view and also calls attention to other aspects of the change process which is crucial to success in most situations. (p. 25)

Is OD involved in total quality management (TQM)?

One definition of TQM describes it as a "cooperative form of operating an organization in a way that relies on the talents of both labor and management to continually improve quality and productivity using teams and facts in decision making" (Schmidt & Finnegan, 1993, p. 172). TQM represents a considerable conceptual shift from a production/technical-oriented philosophy to a more humanistic approach that values quality and, at the same time, the psychosocial needs of the members working in the organization. When people are happy with their work situation, when they feel they are valued by the organization for their contributions, their self-esteem is increased, and they are more committed to the quality of what they produce and to the growth of the organization.

Some of the basic concepts underlying TQM that need to be understood by both managers and employees are summarized from Schmidt and Finnegan (1993) and McLaughlin and Kaluzny (1990):

1. The organization is a complex system of suppliers and customers. Customers and suppliers may be both internal (one department giving or receiving resources from another department) or external (exchange of resources among organizations, plus delivery to the ultimate customer or client).
2. The organization is customer driven. *Quality* means meeting the requirements of the customer.
3. There is continuous and relentless improvement in the total process, not just improvement of individuals or specific work units. The organization is a learning organization that is dependent on its members' becoming increasingly competent and creative.
4. There is meaningful participation of all personnel. Teams and work groups are the primary vehicles for planning and problem solving.
5. There needs to be a climate of openness and trust at all levels. This climate is facilitated by thoughtful responses from top management to suggestions made by employees.
6. There is a rigorous process flow and statistical analysis and evaluation of all ongoing activities. The main statistical tools include Pareto diagrams (a special form of vertical bar graph designed to help determine which problems to solve and in what order to solve them), histograms, scatter diagrams, flowcharts, run and trend charts, and control charts. Use of these measurement and evaluation tools takes the guesswork out of decision making.
7. There is a recognition and an application of underlying psychosocial principles affecting individuals and groups within the organization.
8. TQM will make use of quality circles (see section on QC, above).

The theory and methods of OD are intimately congruent with TQM. They embrace group dynamics, training and development for employees and managers, employee involvement, corporate culture change, and leadership issues.

The values of TQM are humanistic/participative: listening to and understanding customer needs, working collaboratively with others, being a good team member. The challenges that TQM presents to organization members are to be a good supplier, customer, coach, team leader, team member, process observer, planner, problem solver, communicator, and listener; to keep learning and improving; and to increase one's understanding of TQM.

How does OD apply to total quality improvement (TQI)? Is the application different from TQM?

The American Productivity and Quality Center (1992) defines *total quality improvement* (TQI) as the organizations reliance on human resources to control and improve the following: (a) services and materials supplied to the organization, (b) the processes that result in the organizations' products and services, and (c) the satisfaction of customer needs (Section 1, p. 10). The TQI definition is broken down into *quantitative methods*—using statistical tools to measure or analyze data (not opinions) on which to make decisions, and *human resources*—using all the people in the organization. These human resources work in *teams* using the data and tools to improve the quality of supplying, processing, and customer satisfaction. There is also an emphasis on continuous improvement, employee involvement, and the use of a variety of measuring tools. TQI rests on principles of communication, teamwork, effective problem solving, and statistics. The statistical methods in TQI or TQM are not exactly the same as those used by behavioral scientists (e.g., correlational techniques, analysis of variance, factor analysis). They are tied more to production and services (e.g., bar charts, scattergrams; see Item 6 in the previous section).

There appears to be very little difference, if any, between total quality management (TQM), described above, and TQI. Both appear to have the same methods, theory, and goals, and to utilize the basic concepts of Deming (1986), Juran (1988, 1989), and Crosby (1979, 1984), among others. What we have said about how OD applies to TQM also applies here. OD theory and technologies are obviously appropriate to and intimately involved in communication, teamwork, problem solving, and employee involvement. The emphasis on statistics and measuring tools for analysis of data in TQM and TQI is not central to OD practices except to evaluate progress and degree of goal achievement. In OD's current expansion, however, that gap is closing. There is a danger, however, that TQI and TQM will become task oriented and mechanistic if the people-oriented processes are given little or no attention. Many programs like TQM, TQI, and MBO have greater potential for success if they are set in an OD climate.

 **7**

OD and the Manager/ Administrator

How can OD help me in my job as a manager/administrator?

There are many ways in which an OD program can be useful to a manager in his or her daily work. Several that are general are listed below. Other more specific uses may emerge and vary from manager to manager, depending upon the nature of the work situation and the leadership style of the manager. The potential benefits of an OD program include:

- Raising the level of consciousness about interpersonal, team, and organizational effectiveness (i.e., helping people increase their awareness of the "process" involved in such things as communication, interpersonal feedback, group problem solving, leadership styles, decision making, and goal setting).
- Clarifying work unit goals with team members and defining their role functions and how they will contribute to goal achievement.
- Improving skills as an effective manager, communicator, team leader, and organizational facilitator.
- Creating a system in which the needs and desires of individual employees can be brought to fruition within an organizational context and, at the same time, facilitate the organization's mission.
- Helping the individual consider or relate to some basic dimensions of personal change and learning; that is, (a) developing awareness of one's present state—perceptions, feelings, beliefs, and attitudes; (b) providing a means for looking at how one's attitudes affect one's behavior, or how one's behavior reflects one's attitudes; (c) reevaluating attitudes that lead to ineffective behaviors, and experimenting with different behaviors consistent with new or

changed attitudes; and (d) learning and integrating new behaviors more appropriate to the present situation in which the manager finds him- or herself.

Managers perform a variety of functions: administration, management program implementation, service or product delivery, learning, supervising, planning, problem solving, team leading, public relations, and so forth. Fundamental to their work are their skills and competencies as social change agents. Developing managers' ability to weld these complex functions into an effective whole is the area in which the OD consultant can be useful.

How can OD help a manager deal with more programs, more work, and fewer people?

OD consultation can help in two ways that are interdependent: improving productivity by increasing effectiveness of the way people do the work, and assessing priorities. As a consequence of developing skills in OD (e.g., problem identification or diagnosis, planning, implementation, and evaluation), the issue may not necessarily be *fewer* or *more* people, but rather working more effectively with the people who already work in the programs. This process is accomplished best when the people doing the work are involved in the problem-solving sequence. Managers can utilize work teams and participate in the team's work as facilitators and as contributors, making available to the group their own expertise. It is important, however, that managers empower team members to participate in the decision making, avoiding undue influence based on their authority as the "boss." The other issue is evaluating more realistically where the priorities lie in relation to the organizational mission and accepting the limitations under which people work. Again, as a team project, OD consultation can help people look at the process by which priorities are set (if at all) and assess how much of their work is really not necessary (e.g., tradition, ineffective group or cultural norms not relevant to the mission of the organization), unnecessarily time consuming, or just a waste of time.

How can OD help me work with my subordinates, superiors, and peers/colleagues?

We will address these questions by prefacing them with two points of view that reflect behavioral science and OD values. Whether an individual manager is looking up, down, or sideways, it is useful to keep in mind some concepts that will apply to all members of an organization. In a number of our own workshops that involved "what motivates employees," the items that were ranked high were very similar for all levels. That is, items reflecting the top part of Maslow's hierarchy of needs, such as belonging and love, esteem and self-actualization (self-fulfillment), were ranked high regardless of whether the participants were employees, supervisors, or managers. When predicting the rankings of lower level employees, however, the supervisors and managers thought that their subordinates would not rank these needs high. The caveat here is, when looking up, down, or sideways, do not be blindsided by rank or position.

As far back as 1950, many of the OD principles were gaining popularity and, more important, credibility. Homans (1950) described three "givens" in his concept of the small group that are certainly applicable to work teams and team leaders. These givens are:

1. *Contribution opportunity*—"extent to which an individual's 'required activities' are not so highly programmed that no room is left for the individual's contribution to them" (Homans, 1950, cited in Clark, 1971, p. 107). Assembly lines lack this feature.

2. *Interaction opportunity*—"extent to which an individual's 'required interactions' do not limit him from getting together, on a social as well as a task basis, with others" (Homans, 1950, cited in Clark, 1971, p. 107).

3. *Influence opportunity*—"a function of leadership behavior, [it] has an effect on an individual's motivation. . . . When we are closely controlled or highly programmed, this violates our expectations of satisfying superior-subordinate behavior" (Homans, 1950, cited in Clark, 1971, pp. 107-108).

Sheldon Davis of TRW Systems (cited in Grossman, 1974, pp. 121, 122) put behavioral science principles to work in developing several guidelines for a more effective employer/employee relationship, some of which are summarized here: The individual is important; trust individuals with minimum rules and controls; develop a society of peers rather than a rigid hierarchy; delegate a great deal downward so that large numbers of people end up with responsible tasks; and assume that work ought to be personally rewarding, meaningful, and fun.

As far as working with *subordinates* is concerned, OD can offer training in dealing with people creatively, can help look at different ways to evaluate work with subordinates, and can provide support for change toward increased effectiveness. The more a supervisor or manager is in touch with his or her own personal/interpersonal style, power, assets, and liabilities, the more this awareness will help him or her, in the final analysis, to deal more effectively with all people with whom he or she has contact and, more specifically, subordinates. In addition, the training that goes with OD can help to keep a manager more aware of and open to the values and needs of the younger generation of workers entering and moving up in the organization. Over the past 30-plus years, there has been a change of values among young workers—a change in the way they view work and its meaning in a larger social context. Some of the shifts involve a concern for quality rather than just quantity; interdependence rather than independence of nations, institutions, and individuals; living in harmony with nature rather than dominating it; cooperation rather than competition; "being" rather than just doing and planning; consideration of social justice and equity over the primacy of technology; aspirations of self-realization and learning over dictates of organizational convenience; participation over authoritarianism and dogmatism; diversity and pluralism over uniformity and centralization; and work as purpose and self-fulfillment over work as hard and unavoidable (Yankelovich, 1981). These newer values, like OD values, reflect a work philosophy of humanism. Managers who hold too strictly to a narrow and more traditional view of their work may not reach many of the newer type of employees, who are a product of an era characterized by chronic and rapid technical and social change.

The discussion in the above paragraphs also applies to working with one's *superiors.* In addition, the manager may be an OD consultant to his or her superior by developing skills that will enable him or her to function in a variety of roles that can be useful in meeting the needs of the superior and/or others in upper level management positions. For example, it might be possible to meet with superiors in order to clarify the needs and expectations both have of each other, or to share concepts and technologies concerning team building, problem solving, or program evaluation. In those organizations in which OD has been most effective, upper management is coming to see supervisors and managers as valuable resources with important information and perspectives that need to be seriously considered in making decisions and in achieving organizational goals. This is particularly true of managers who have ideas on how new procedures and programs may be instituted, using knowledge and skills gained from previous exposure to OD theory and methods. An ideal work relationship between a manager and his or her superior is one that is mutually supportive and caring.

As for working with one's *peers or colleagues,* managers can operate more effectively as a team by increasing collegiality through mutual personal and professional support, by developing skills in working together more effectively, by utilizing (not competing with) each other's resources in dealing with common problems, and by taking an active stance toward accomplishing this goal. In many organizations it is not unusual for managers/administrators to feel —and be—isolated from their colleagues, cut off from mutual consultation and teamwork by barriers of low trust, competitiveness, physical distance, and historical norms of separation. Many department heads have a tendency to expend all their energies working with their own employees and departmental tasks to the exclusion of relating to other work unit personnel. This is particularly true if they do not delegate well and micromanage rather than utilizing a team approach. This self-imposed separation further exacerbates their sense of isolation and fosters a narrow perspective of the organization's functioning. OD can help in creating useful and facilitative bridges between and among colleagues.

If, through OD concepts and practices, the managers have a keener sense of the organization of which they are a part and its internal dynamics, then they can work more effectively with their fellow managers. For example, in many organizations, managers work more effectively when they have a clear sense of the organization's mission and how each other's work units contribute to that goal, when they cooperate on solving interdepartmental problems, when they work in task groups rather than working on assignments alone, when they feel free to express themselves and confront their differences by hearing each other out and getting clear on what was said, when they are open about examining their own leadership style and its impact on employees and other managers, and when they have regular useful and productive team meetings.

How can OD help me to exert influence in my organization?

Part of an OD program will usually involve examining one's leadership style or style of influence. What one has to offer may be extremely valuable to another employee, manager, or executive. How one does it, however, may create resistance, indifference, or receptivity in the other person. An autocratic style of influence may arouse resistance and create dependency (Theory X). A participative style of influence empowers others and fosters interdependence, responsibility, and ownership (Theory Y). A laissez-faire style of influence, research indicates, creates frustration in employees—with no guidelines or directions from the leader, employees have no sense of what is wanted from them. OD philosophy espouses a participative, team-oriented approach to organizations and management practices. Managers become consultants to others and assume the role of change agents. In addition, the personal and professional resources each manager brings to bear as a consultant to a subordinate, peer, or superior, and the quality of his or her relationship with them, will largely determine the degree of his or her influence. It is important, whenever and wherever possible, to develop the types of relationships whereby one can receive some constructive feedback on one's leadership style and skills of exerting influence. In any event, an OD program can help one define these issues more clearly.

What does OD have to do with the manager's vocation/profession (e.g., how is OD central to what he or she is supposed to do)?

Although OD may have very little to do with a particular vocation or profession as viewed in a narrow or technical sense (best left to a vocational counselor), it can facilitate the clarification and enhancement of the vocational function of the individual as it relates to the organization in several ways:

- OD can help individuals to clarify their personal/vocational goals and promote implementation of these goals within the context of the organizational framework.
- OD has values that are consonant with many vocational/professional values (i.e., increasing one's level of competence, being effective in one's work, being open in one's interpersonal relations, facilitating clearer communication, increasing the level of trust among individuals, increasing commitment to organizational goals while maintaining personal integrity, and humanizing the organization so that organizational goals are not achieved at the expense of the individual's feelings of self-worth or self-esteem).
- OD can help individuals examine the extent to which their values are reflected in their everyday behavior.
- Differences among individuals, more than sameness, enrich our perspective of the world. If this statement is a reflection of the value system of the organization, then OD can help individuals look at the congruence of their personal value system and their effectiveness with people who hold values different from their own.

We have operational responsibility but no managerial accountability; therefore, how does OD apply to us?

The question arouses some speculations. Many managers, particularly supervisors, are evaluated on their ability to manage the work of the employees in their department or work unit, and that is where their responsibility ends. Does this mean that managers and supervisors interpret these responsibilities as the limits of their authority and power, and that the more managerial functions are handled elsewhere? Does it mean that they cannot promote employees in their unit, move people around, evaluate their performance, hire or fire people, and so forth without permission from higher level management? Part of the problem is that although many supervisors *feel* or *think* that they do not have this type of authority or accountability, they may never have really tested that assumption. In addition, managers are constantly, if implicitly, being evaluated on their interpersonal and leadership effectiveness at work and may not have given this aspect of their work role sufficient weight as a source of influence. In an OD program, issues such as role clarification (other related techniques: role analysis, role negotiation, role prescription) and responsibilities would be addressed. In a team setting, communication among managers, supervisors, and higher level management would be facilitated by an OD practitioner so that interpersonal and leadership issues could be worked through. Data for team meetings might include a diagnosis of team functioning and satisfaction of team members. The problems, if any, of responsibility and accountability would certainly surface during these work team meetings.

Can managers really be helped to change their managerial style after years of doing it one way?

Yes, but only if *they* want to change it. The philosophy behind OD makes the assumption that learning is a lifelong process and that given information (feedback) about one's leadership style, under conditions relatively free of threat or pressure to change, individuals can make choices about the direction in which they want to move. Thus, individuals can increase their awareness of their own style and determine what aspects of it they want to change or what behaviors they want to maintain and build upon. Part of the function of OD consultation is to help build a climate in which individuals feel free to express themselves and see the value of exchanging this type of information.

Now that we have said the above, we would like to add that changing one's interpersonal, managerial, or leadership style is much easier said than done. We have spent a lifetime developing our lifestyles and have a considerable amount of emotional investment in maintaining our own status quo. Once we have decided what we want to change about the way we interrelate and lead, the old behavior does not simply disappear. The new behaviors must be practiced, practiced, and practiced. In a climate supportive of our new behaviors, temporary slips into old behavior patterns can be fed back to us. Another factor hindering the integration of new leadership styles can come from others in the work setting. Behaving differently makes us less predictable to others, who may now, in many subtle ways, attempt to keep us as we were. This phenomenon happens frequently in therapeutic programs in which one member of a family is in therapy and the changes in his or her behavior are met with resistance by other family members. Even though the behaviors of the family member were ineffectual, he or she was at least predictable and, as a consequence, more comfortable and less threatening. In any event, in an OD program, changes in managerial style and responses to these changes can be monitored by the consultant and other team members.

Could the OD effort involve family members also?

To the extent that family life is a concern of the organization's mission (as in religious and social organizations), yes. The family, as a system, has its own set of dynamics not unlike those of other small groups in which each individual is an integral part. To consider the manager completely independent of his or her family is to violate good OD principles about interdependence of systems. Sometimes the family of the manager feels involved with his or her work, particularly when other families are involved; certainly, in these situations family pressures do affect the manager at work in one way or another. Family involvement can be beneficial when approached with openness, sensitivity, and forethought. Some companies integrate family members into the general information network by such practices as sending reports, company magazines, special letters from management, and special pages for wives, husbands, and families. The content of this information is relevant to the organization. Open houses and family picnics are other ways organizations reach out to families. These efforts may be initiated through an OD program that sees the families of workers as a potential resource and support for the members of the organization. It is important, however, to be cognizant of the types of problems, such as conflicts of interest, that may arise when more than one system is making demands upon the same individual. Family involvement can reduce the potential for these conflicts to occur.

How can an individual manager or administrator contribute to an OD program in his or her organization?

Managers can contribute to an OD program in their organization in several ways, but all of them require a proactive stance on the manager's part. It is important for managers to understand the OD process and to be involved in the diagnosis and planning phases in order to make more effective contributions to the OD program. Some of the ways managers can develop themselves and make contributions are:

- Getting consultation from a consultant and other managers to learn more effective uses of the self in work relationships. Over and above skills and techniques are the managers themselves, what they bring personally to the organization and to their work associates.
- Reading pertinent and available OD material.
- Obtaining more training through the National Training Laboratories Institution for Applied Behavioral Science (NTL) Institute or similar programs.
- Becoming more involved as part of a management team with higher level officers. In this way the manager becomes a link not only with his or her own team of subordinates but with managers in other departments. The manager also gets a broader perspective on the organization's mission and how all units contribute to it.
- Attending meetings, in addition to those above, and helping to develop more effective ways of conducting and participating in them. This means, for example, a willingness to speak up when the agenda is bogging down because of ineffective task and maintenance behaviors, when underlying tensions are not being addressed.
- Becoming an effective advocate for change when one sees the necessity for such change.
- Not accepting things as they are (status quo), but striving for continuous improvement (see Chapter 6, total quality management).

Some of the above items obviously require energy, commitment, courage to take risks, and the "courage to be imperfect."

OD Within a Subsystem of an Organization

Is my department an "organization"?

This question is typically asked by managers wondering whether OD can be done solely within their own particular department that is part of a larger organization. What confuses the issue is that the term *organization development* may be interpreted as the total organization or the company for which they work. For example, we seldom use the expression *department development*, even though this is a legitimate term. The answer to the question is "yes." A department has most of the features of the total organization, although it is smaller in scope and size. It consists of a group of people joined by a common identity; working within a common framework; holding, to a marked degree, a common set of work values; and working toward a common goal or mission. Departments may be large or small, relatively self-contained or intimately bound with other departments within the much larger structure. A large department may have several smaller work units or teams. For example, a large hospital may have several services (departments) that are further broken down into wards, each having its own treatment team (see Chapter 1, Figure 1.1). Individuals within departments may have a number of loyalties outside the department, such as union, professional, and managerial ties and affiliations. These loyalties may sometimes create conflicts of interest, as when a psychologist on a ward treatment team has been scheduled by her service chief to attend meetings that conflict with her ward staff meetings. In addition, many large organizations, particularly of an international scope, may have identical or related departments widely dispersed in different geographical regions. In essence, a department is an organization within an organization.

On the other hand, no department is an entity in and of itself, independent of other departments or of the organization of which it is a part. It relates to other departments as customer or supplier of resources and services. Much of what can be done by an OD program for the organization can be done for a department or for a work unit or team within a department. The process is very similar (see Chapters 1 and 2). The manager and the OD consultant can work together to diagnose current functioning of the department, plan and implement interventions, and evaluate outcomes. Members of work teams would also be involved in this process. From the description above, it is obvious that the OD efforts may also involve relationships with other departments and with the organization as a whole. Much of the early work of OD practitioners was done with smaller units or subsystems of larger organizations.

What are some possible OD goals for my department?

This question can be addressed from two perspectives: the relationship of the department to the larger organization, and the relationships and functioning within the department itself. These two perspectives are not independent of each other. In the first situation, there needs to be some assessment concerning the department's contribution to the organization's mission. If the department is performing an adequate job in relation to the organization, a departmental goal might be improvement of departmental performance. The goal of continuous improvement is primary to total quality management, and TQM and its technology may be incorporated here. If the department is not performing adequately, then the problem may lie within the department. The initial goal would be to diagnose the situation, identify the problem areas, plan ways to address the problem, implement the intervention, and evaluate the outcomes. This OD process would help to clarify the department's present level of functioning and facilitate the setting of clear and relevant goals. In answer to the question, a short-term goal would be to assess the effectiveness of the department's current functioning. The longer term goal would be to increase the department's contribution to the productivity and quality of work toward the organization's goals.

A general goal adopted by some executives is for managers to become primary agents for change, not only for their own departments but for the organization's community. They already play the role of consultant to their own department and can develop mutual consultant relationships with other managers. In this way they will be exerting more influence on, and becoming more involved with, all levels of the organization.

Another goal for many managers is to empower their employees by giving them more responsibility, acknowledging their contributions to the team effort, and removing barriers to their creativity. Under these conditions, employees develop a strong sense of loyalty to and identification with the organization. See Chapters 1 and 4 for other possible goals, and for a description of what an effective work team looks like along a number of dimensions. In Chapter 4, an organization and/or an OD program that is working effectively versus one that is not is characterized. Items from these lists can also be used as goals for an OD program in a department. One word of caution is needed. In setting goals and implementing them for a department, the manager has to take into consideration the impact of change on other departments. This is particularly true if there is an exchange of resources and services between or among the departments.

An OD program is one means of helping managers decide for themselves in what direction they want to move and what types of objectives they want to establish for their departments. Many managers are engaged in a struggle to develop a sense of mission and identity within their own organization. In these times of turbulence, cultural change, and shifting work values (what Vaill, 1989a, called "permanent whitewater"), the present role of the manager is ambiguous, and consequently in need of serious clarification. In that unfolding struggle, the skills of OD can be very helpful.

What would an OD program look like for my department?

The OD program for a department consists of supplying consultation to the manager and employees to assist them in examining their structure, function, and process so that they may define and implement their mission more effectively. The consultation may also be geared toward helping the department find viable methods for communicating its mission to other departments and to the organization's community. In short, the OD program is designed to help the department become a more effective and influential component in the organization.

The OD program also focuses on helping managers and supervisors increase their competence as professional leaders and administrators, promoting cohesive, well-functioning work teams, and assisting department members in acquiring skills to bring about effective personal and organizational change. One aspect of personal change, for example, might be to help managers examine their own leadership style and to see to what extent their values are consistent with that style as it is reflected in their everyday interpersonal transactions. Characteristics of an effective team that may reflect a manager's style of leadership is described in Chapter 1.

An OD program within a department would look like an OD program for the organization. It would contain many of the elements described earlier in Chapters 1 and 2, or in programs involving quality management. Of course, the program would be in attenuated form and limited in scope compared to a total organization OD program. But a departmental OD effort could still have significant impact on the organization's goals.

What does OD have to do with interdepartmental relations?

Throughout these responses, we have frequently addressed the issue of the interdependence of subsystems; that is, how changes in one department or work unit affect other departments or work units. Departments cannot operate independently in an organization. It is important to examine the nature of subsystems and what happens when they interface with each other. For this response, we will introduce concepts derived from intergroup theory.

Organizations consist of suborganizations or subsystems that need to work together to achieve the overall goals of the organization. The subsystems include departments, divisions, services, and work teams, as well as night and day shifts, staff and line, management and labor, engineering and production, sales and manufacturing, and headquarters and plants or field stations. In addition, informal groupings may occur along lines of race, gender, ethnicity, age, and alternative lifestyles. These units or groups may develop norms, standards, values, and goals different from other groups'. That is, departments or divisions may develop their own individual work cultures within the broader organizational culture. When these groups work together on some issue or task, dynamics and stereotypes may develop between the groups that may inhibit or facilitate productive cooperation and task accomplishment.

Tensions in interdepartmental and intergroup relationships can be created when individuals institute changes in one department without considering their impact on another department; individuals in one department, either unwittingly or out of loyalty to their own department, express an attitude or take some action that frustrates or antagonizes another department; work standards in one department (e.g., meeting deadlines, production rates, scheduling) may create problems in another department, the work productivity of which is dependent on the first department; departments get into competition with each other because of scarcity of resources wanted by both; or there is preferential treatment of one group over another. If the conditions that create these tensions are not reduced or resolved, intergroup conflict may increase, and departments may get locked into mutually destructive interactions. Under conditions of intergroup conflict, some of the following conditions may occur:

1. Each group forms negative stereotypes of the other group. Communication is filtered through these stereotypes that distort each group's perceptions of the other.
2. Communication is decreased, distorted, or censored:
   a. Members of one group do not want to hear the other group's viewpoint, preferring to listen only to what supports their own position.
   b. Employees see only differences and ignore similarities between their group's viewpoint and that of the other group.
   c. Reasonable requests from the other group are heard as "demands."
3. Hostility between groups increases; each group sees the other as antagonistic.
4. Each group withholds resources from the other group. Products are not as good or creative as when groups share and pool their resources.
5. Groups develop win/lose strategies; energy, creativity, and resources are expended in trying to make the other group lose; feelings are generated that tend to feed and perpetuate nonproductive interactions.
6. Interaction may decrease, and the two groups may withdraw from each other into a standoff position or a position of "peaceful" coexistence and conflict avoidance "at any cost."

The manager or OD consultant will usually work on intergroup relations after some work on team building with either one or both of the groups has been accomplished. A team or group needs to resolve its own internal relationship issues, attain some cohesion, and develop process skills before it can effectively handle intergroup issues. Otherwise, the attempts to deal with intergroup conflict may create greater tensions and difficulties within each group and further disrupt any fragile relationships that already exist.

In an effort to resolve interdepartmental or intergroup problems, managers can get together and help both their groups embark on a program of intergroup development that involves increasing communication between their respective groups or departments and coordinating both groups' efforts so that responsibility is more effectively shared in achieving organizational goals. Some of the strategies for creating more constructive and cooperative intergroup relationships may involve the following concepts and actions:

- Helping both groups to understand the conditions in their relationship that foster antagonism and nonproductive competition.
- Identifying common goals that provide an impetus for resolving intergroup problems.
- Helping both groups to examine the behavioral culture of both groups.
- Helping both groups to examine the stereotypes they have of each other and to get a clear understanding of what they mean.
- Helping each group to accept these stereotypes as "real" for the other group and to examine their own behaviors in light of these stereotypes to see to what extent these behaviors contribute to or perpetuate the stereotypes. For example, individuals in both groups may tend to act on attitudes, values, or vested interests that may be viewed by the other group as against their own best interests.
- Developing action plans for identifying the key divisive issues, reducing them, and moving both groups in a cooperative direction.
- Helping each group to understand that sharing and pooling resources rather than withholding them, and channeling energy into cooperative efforts rather than draining them off into competitive struggles, increases the energy level of both groups (cumulative effect of sharing and pooling resources) and creates conditions for more creative problem solving.
- Helping both groups to understand that achieving good intergroup relations, like team building, is an ongoing effort that requires continuous monitoring and checking. It is also extremely important to develop a commitment from each group to this process.

For further reading on the subject, see Blake, Shepard, and Mouton (1964), Likert and Likert (1976), and Walton (1987, pp. 119-153).

Who is responsible for OD in my department or in my organization?

The chief executive officer is ultimately responsible for the OD program. He or she is the chief or ultimate recipient, ideally speaking, of the consultant's services for the achievement of the organization's goals. The first contact may be with the department manager who is requesting assistance. The manager may have already discussed the situation with the CEO. In many cases, managers may have the freedom to use their own funds at their own discretion. In large organizations, the CEO may be remote from the department and need only to be apprised of what is going on and of its progress. It is best, however, when the chief executive officer or his or her delegate and the manager fully collaborate in what the consultant does. As the three of them work together, they can broaden the consultant's contacts to others who will be affected by any change program. When an OD effort is focusing on a particular department or organizational unit, the role of the CEO may be more supportive than active in the program. Each manager, supervisor, or employee has the opportunity to participate in the program. The extent of their participation and acceptance of the program will be related to their understanding of the concepts and philosophy of OD and to the extent to which they accept responsibility for their own behavior as it affects the work unit or team. Their support of the OD program will be in proportion to how much they experience that something "good" is happening. Top- and middle-level authority must be actively supportive, however, if the OD program is to be effective in its impact on the organization.

Harrison (in press) described three levels of top management commitment to an OD program. The lowest level is giving permission for change to occur. The second level is giving support and encouragement for the change effort. The highest level involves participation in the change program. This last level is seldom achieved.

Is an OD program a one-shot or time-limited program?

The question of a "quick fix" for organizational problems has been addressed previously, but it may be useful to elaborate on the consequences of a one-shot program. The time perspective will be different for a department as opposed to the total organization. In the first instance, a manager may learn enough from an OD consultant to carry on after a reasonable amount of consultation time and follow-up evaluation. An OD program with the total organization is more complex, and changes are more gradual and less likely to emerge as measurable items in a short time.

A major value of OD consultation is the philosophy that any program has to be long term in order to be effective. One-shot or time-limited OD efforts have very little impact and no lasting effect, particularly on large and complex organizations. Indeed, one-shot efforts may be detrimental in that they build expectations that may never be met and consequently result in a negative attitude toward any future OD programs. OD programs need top-level support to survive. OD is consistent with a growing applied behavioral science thrust in many organizations, which facilitates a supportive climate for OD among upper and middle management. As more and more managers and supervisors are trained in concepts and policies of OD, the program will develop a momentum of its own. One of the typical long-range goals of an OD program is that it will become institutionalized and rely primarily on internal resources. Experience with many short-term "faddish" innovations has biased many organizations against change efforts. A well-planned program, with top-level support and provisions and with sufficient time to develop internal resources and to allow progress at the organization's own pace, usually proves durable and is taken seriously by people in the organization.

What can an OD program do for us that we can't do for ourselves?

Probably nothing if management really chooses to do it. Using an external OD consultant can help the organization to overcome inertia and resistance to change. A fresh, "outside" view is often useful, along with the skills, resources, and experience that the external consultant brings to the task. OD consultation is a vehicle that can help managers evaluate their present situation to see if they are meeting their personal and organizational needs. Because managers are part of the process consultants need to observe, consultants can provide information not readily available to managers from their own employees and colleagues. Consultants can help managers develop skills for collecting this type of information for themselves and gradually free them of their dependence on the consultants. OD is a vehicle for encouraging self-help, in which consultants gradually work themselves out of a job by developing people within the organization to do their work.

Depending upon the size and complexity of the OD program, however, the ideal just described may take a long time to achieve. In essence, external OD consultants are creating internal OD consultants or units. In his paper "Strategy Guidelines for an Internal Organization Development Unit,"

Harrison (in press) offered 13 guidelines, abbreviated below, to help managers who choose to do OD for themselves:

1. Work *with* the forces in the organization that are supportive of change and improvement, rather than working against those who are defensive and resistant.

2. Try to develop 'critical mass' in each change project, a self-sustaining organization improvement process that is motivated and powered from within the system which is changing.

3. When working with a given system, try to find multiple entry points into it: a variety of people, groups, processes and problems with which contact can be made and to which help may be given.

4. Look for 'felt needs,' problems recognized by managers that can be dealt with by OD techniques and processes.

5. Wherever possible, work with relatively healthy parts of the organization, which have the will and the resources to improve. Avoid being seduced or pressured into working on 'lost causes,' individuals or groups that have lost the ability to cope with the situation as it is.

6. Work with individuals and groups that have as much freedom and discretion in managing their own operations as possible. It profits nothing to work out an agreed change with a manager who turns out not to have the latitude to carry it out.

7. Try to obtain appropriate and realistic levels of involvement in the program of the OD unit on the part of top management.

8. Try to establish direct communication and contact with all levels of the organization. Try to develop customs and accepted practices of operating that exempt OD unit members from following normal bureaucratic channels or the 'chain of command.'

9. Develop confidence and credibility on the part of organization members through situations in which the OD unit's unique expertise shows to best advantage.

10. Don't be afraid to ask to be involved in activities in which you feel you may be able to make a contribution.

11. Make known what the OD unit is doing, particularly when there are successes to report (but only with the client's permission, of course).

12. Use outside consultants in ways that enhance, rather than compete, with the credibility of OD unit members.

13. Link together people who are working to improve organization functioning, so their activities reinforce and complement one another.

How can OD help to motivate my staff—help them to feel more identified with the corporate staff and to help me to upgrade their professional caliber ?

The two questions are related. We do not have to stretch a point to say that upgrading employees' skills and competencies increases their motivation to function more effectively in their work situation. It is incumbent upon managers to provide incentives to their employees to continuously improve their work performance. It is also good business. The more competently workers perform, the more productive they are in their work setting. What are some of these incentives? Employees feel valued when their contributions are solicited and given thoughtful consideration by management. Even when contributions are not accepted, employees will respond positively if they are given a reason why their particular suggestion was rejected, and if they are encouraged to continue offering their ideas and other contributions.

Related to employees' contributions is how much influence they want and have in what happens on the job. Do they participate in decisions that affect their work life? At team meetings, are they being listened to and asked for their thoughts and feelings about what is being discussed? Being influential does not mean that employees get everything they ask for, but it means that they are considered valuable assets to the team, department, or organization. The feelings that stem from being influential increase self-esteem and commitment to the department and to the organization.

People are social animals, and employees are people first and workers second. Many of our social needs are met on the job with work associates. It would not be surprising to discover that most of our social activities outside of the work situation are with coworkers. Managers who create a work climate that allows employees to interact with each other on nonwork topics are facilitating the fulfillment of workers' social needs.

Managers who want to upgrade the caliber of their staffs need to encourage and make available opportunities to attend training and educational events such as workshops, seminars, visiting lecturers, and in-house sessions provided by OD consultants. The latter events can provide a broader perspective of the dynamics of the work situation and the development of process skills and OD theory and philosophy.

Under these conditions, employee identification with the organization and the corporate staff will be greatly enhanced. The message to employees from above is that managers have some understanding of what makes for satisfactory, meaningful, pleasant, and productive work conditions, and are willing to provide opportunities for employees' personal and professional growth. In addition, managers can provide the link between the employees and the corporate staff by demystifying the image of corporate officers. The OD practitioner can help managers identify what employees need, what they feel is important to them on the job, what they want more of in their work situation, and what else it takes to increase their work satisfaction and commitment. Both OD consultants and managers can explore, plan, and implement the means to accomplish the goals identified in the above question.

Can OD help the manager do a better job in decisions regarding hiring, firing, and promotions?

In a department or organization in which an OD program is in progress, these issues are addressed as part of the OD process. The consultants can help managers set up structures such as participative groups that may take over the responsibility of hiring, monitoring unit members' progress or lack of it, and developing criteria by which individuals are promoted. Hiring and promotion are usually thought of as positive events. For managers, however, they represent critical decisions that have impact on other employees.

Managers can reduce the anxiety-provoking aspects of these activities through shared responsibility with group unit or team members. For example, in some organizations, participative groups take over most of these responsibilities for their own work unit. Who knows better than they what is required to be an effective or productive worker in that particular unit? This is not to say that managers should absent themselves from these decisions. They should be intimately involved, but not in a dominating or autocratic way.

One of managers' most painful experiences is that of having to fire someone. In an OD climate that is open, confronting, and supportive, poor performance is addressed early, allowing time for possible correction. Feedback is ongoing, not delayed until the situation is beyond repair. In many work situations, however, the employee's termination comes as a surprise followed by strong feelings of resentment.

In today's climate of economic uncertainty, many employees are faced with layoffs due not to their own incompetence but to plant closings, mergers, downsizing, and other organizational crises. These crises can be devastating to the individual's sense of confidence, security, and self-esteem. In organizations faced with these crises, OD practitioners have been involved in exploring options to reduce the cutbacks or to manage them in a humane and helpful way. Some of these options are described below (see French & Bell, 1990):

- Organizations used facilitators and group methods to ease the anxieties and disappointments of those being laid off and to help people plan for seeking employment elsewhere. The employees were also notified weeks ahead of time.

- Using groups again, the leader and group members helped each other to face up to the realities of the cutbacks and to reduce perceptual distortions. They also used the group to make plans and to cope with termination.

- Several organizations used devices to avoid or reduce cutbacks and to accomplish cost reduction through normal attrition, retraining and transfers, curtailment of hiring, and offers of early retirement.

These crisis situations are integral parts of organizational realities. They cannot be wished away or dealt with through a variety of denial maneuvers. They must be confronted directly and openly in as humane a way as possible. This approach is congruent with OD philosophy.

What should be my first OD project?

The first OD project should be one with a high probability of success. That means it should be relatively uncomplicated, manageable in scope, and supported by higher level management. (See the guidelines for an internal OD unit in this chapter.) A manager who is willing to take some risks is not helped by meeting with failure on his or her first try. In some organizations, OD has gotten a negative reputation because people took on more than they could effectively manage and failed in their first attempts. It is to be hoped that the consultant will monitor the process to keep the manager out of deep water.

The first step, of course, is to look around the department to see if anything needs fixing. With the help of an OD consultant, a needs assessment can be conducted to ascertain the current status of the department. The data collected from this assessment may reveal some leads as to what needs to be explored in greater depth. Employees can also contribute to the collection of this information, which, in turn, is fed back to them. In this way, they get a more objective view of the department and how their individual perceptions compare to those of other employees. In an OD framework, this activity is very similar to a data survey feedback project. The manager presents the findings to the employees, and decisions can be made about how to use the data if discrepancies appear, or, if no problem surfaces, to leave well enough alone. Sometimes when everything looks OK, rather than accept the status quo and do nothing, the manager or the consultant may ask, "Can we do better?" The project of data collection and feedback, incidentally, is an OD project. It can also be a first step to other OD interventions.

OD Consultation

What is an OD consultant?

An OD consultant is a person trained in behavioral sciences, especially organizational behavior, who seeks to help an organization define and clarify its own issues, values, problems, and resources. He or she then collaborates with that organization in developing the best method to mobilize its resources to deal effectively with the issues it has identified. This is done in a way that is consistent with the organization's values. More simply, the consultant is a professional person, usually an outsider, who attempts to help organizations work more effectively.

The OD consultant differs from the expert technical type of consultant in that he or she does not usually address content or task issues (e.g., personnel selection, setting up a computer system, designing or redesigning jobs, setting salary schedules). The expert consultant deals directly with the problem and leaves the scene once it is solved. The OD consultant sees the organization as a system and works with individual, group, and organizational processes. OD consultation is not prescriptive: It usually does not give advice or solve problems for the client, as will happen with the expertise technical approach. One goal of the OD consultant is to help the client become a better problem solver. With many expert consultants, the intervention is a one-shot event. The OD consultant's relationship with the organization is of longer duration, sometimes years. We will deal only with OD consultation. Other definitions of *consultant* may vary to some extent but are basically very similar. Lippitt (1959) produced an early and condensed definition:

The consultation relationship is a *voluntary relationship* between a professional *helper (consultant) and a help-needing system (client),* in which the consultant is attempting to *give help* to the client in the solving of some current or potential *problem* and the relationship is perceived as *temporary* by both parties. Also, the *consultant is an "outsider"* (i.e., not a part of any hierarchial power system in which the client is located). (p. 5)

For Block (1981), a consultant is a person in a position to have some influence over an individual, group, or organization, but who has no direct power to make changes or implement programs (p. 122). Block distinguished between managers and consultants in that managers have direct control over the action, whereas consultants do not. He also saw staff work as consulting work and stated that staff need consulting skills to be effective.

Gallessich (1982) described the consultant relationship as having three components: "A consultant (a specialized professional) assists consultees (agency employees who are also professionals) with work related concerns (the third component)" (p. 6). Consultants are also external to the client organization and have a temporary relationship with it. What a consultant does defines more clearly what a consultant is. We will address this issue in the next section of this chapter.

To Huczynski (1987), consultation was an activity performed by one person in relation to another to help the client apply the resources necessary to solve the problem. The "other" could be a manager, a work team, or the total organization.

An organization is made up of a network of people who interact with each other to achieve the organization's mission. From the top level to the lowest level, *how* people and groups work together is the essence of the consultant's work. Schein (1988) referred to the consultant's work as *process consultation (PC),* defined as "a set of activities on the part of the consultant that helps the client to perceive, understand and act upon the process events that occur in the client's environment in order to improve the situation as defined by the client" (p. 11). Some characteristics of the consultant/client relationship are implicitly or explicitly stated in all definitions:

1. The relationship between the consultant and the client (manager) is voluntary. Either one can withdraw from the relationship if his or her needs are not being met.
2. Both consultant and client become interdependent. They share in all the OD activities, including decision making. Collaboration is the keynote of the relationship.

3. The span of control is discussed and negotiated when there is disagreement.

4. The consultant has no line authority and cannot operate independent of the client. The consultant does have strong influence (derived from expertise status), however, on the OD program decisions and directions.

5. The consultant is primarily concerned with process issues and not content.

6. Communication is two-way, including the mutual sharing of expectations about each other's role and about the program.

7. The consultant sees that part of his or her role is to assist the client to increase OD skills and competencies to develop and implement diagnoses and action plans.

8. When the project is completed, including follow-up and evaluation, to the satisfaction of both consultant and client, the consultant will exit the organization.

9. Finally, there is an assumption that the consultant is competent in OD technology and theory and has some background in the behavioral sciences.

In addition to using outside or external OD consultants, some organizations have internal consultants or change agents on their staff. In Item 7 of the above list, the relationship can be described as one of "consulting pairs," in that managers and consultants share their resources and learn from each other. Consultants provide the view from the outside together with their particular expertise. Managers provide an internal perspective of the organization and its operations. Mutual trust and respect are key ingredients necessary for this relationship.

What does an OD consultant do?

We mentioned in the previous response that what a consultant does also defines what a consultant is. The first part of this response will be general, to be followed by more specific dimensions of the consultant's work.

OD consultants are usually called in when there is a felt need on the part of a client. This need may not be clear to the client but may represent a general feeling that things could be better in the organization and that assistance is needed. The consultant may then help the client to clarify what his or her specific needs are. Although consultants may vary in terms of specific role behaviors, their general approach usually follows a relatively consistent pattern. Consultants are likely to see their first task as becoming deeply familiar with the organization and making explicit to the client what they are learning about the system. This familiarization process may include the use of diagnostic instruments. Consultants may then formulate, with the client, some strategies for making use of what has been learned for the benefit of the organization. To reiterate, consultants help the client gather and analyze data about the organization or subsystem with which they are working, and assist in planning ways of responding to the data. This procedure may involve designing strategies and interventions around the analysis of the data. Consultants then work with the client to evaluate the progress that has been made or the impact of the interventions. The evaluations are usually geared to answer the question, Did the interventions accomplish what they were supposed to accomplish?

Schein (1988) summarized those process events to be observed by the process consultant as

> human actions that occur in the normal flow of work, in the conduct of meetings, in the formal and informal encounters between members of the organization and in the more formal organizational structures. Of particular relevance are the client's own actions and their impact on other people in the organization. (p. 11)

In other words, "The process consultant seeks to give the client insight into what is going on around him, within him, and between him and other people" (p. 11). Let us look at some of the ways in which consultants do their work:

- The consultant establishes an open, mutually sharing relationship with the client, and explores some of the parameters within which they will work.
- The consultant diagnoses the problem and the client's or organization's ability to cope with it. This process includes collecting data through interviews, questionnaires, rating scales, etc.
- The consultant analyzes the data, which may then indicate the need for change. The consultant gives a clear statement of what needs changing and the intentions and expectations from the change. The change goals need to be clear, explicit, and specific so that they are amenable to measurement.
- The consultant and the client (e.g., manager and/or others significantly related to the OD effort) formulate the change plan, which includes proposed interventions, timing, sequence of events, and evaluation of progress.
- At the same time, the consultant helps in the development of an internal climate of openness and trust so that the resources available can be identified, developed, and utilized.

- In the OD effort, the consultant's focus of attention may extend beyond the immediate situation to organizational structures, processes, values, and policies. If the path is open, the consultant can then help the organization to examine its structures, mode of operation, technological and human processes, and responses to environmental changes.

- The consultant can help the client/organization to build and incorporate the skills, concepts, and technologies it needs to diagnose its own problems and increase its problem-solving capabilities. This educational process can be implemented through the consultation program itself, seminars, workshops, group dynamics training (in vivo), group conferences, and individual training (off-site educational events).

What does an OD consultant do for the manager?

Much of what has been described earlier in this chapter applies here, but in the context of a one-on-one relationship rather than a relationship to a generalized client. The OD consultant can help to create relationships and environments in which learning and exploration can take place. In this type of learning environment, managers can be helped to examine their own management style and its impact on the organization, to learn how to collect information about the organization in a way that will facilitate diagnosis of problem areas, to plan action steps to deal with problems surfaced by this diagnosis, and to evaluate the results of their interventions in terms of the mission or goals of the organization. In addition, the consultant can help the managers evaluate to what extent their behavior or actions are consistent with their personal values and with the organization's values and goals. In essence, they become the "consulting pair" described earlier: Both partners learn from each other, each providing a different perspective, one external and the other internal. In some cases, the relationship may take on a mentoring aspect that may involve more personal types of feedback and coaching. A key ingredient here is mutual trust and a strong interest on the consultant's part in the development of the manager.

One important consequence of the consulting pair relationship is that managers become consultants to their own departments. That is, they are both experts (content focus) and consultants (process focus). If part of their goal is to help subordinates become better problem solvers, then the role of consultant is better suited to developing this competence than the formal authoritarian role of the expert. Managers as consultants need to learn which role is most productive for what type of situation. This type of learning is one of the benefits of the consulting pair relationship.

How can I use an OD consultant?

In many contracts, the client has a clear idea of how to use a consultant. On many other occasions, however, "how to use a consultant" needs to be developed with the client. Generally, consultants can be used in all areas of work in which there is a felt or actual need, however vague (i.e., relationships with other managers, superior/subordinate relations, intergroup relations, organizational diagnosis, designing events to deal with problems, developing more effective teamwork, and evaluating programs). What gets worked on initially depends upon the client's perception of the situation and how motivated he or she is to work on these issues. The client's level of motivation is a critical issue. Hiring a consultant may have unexpected results. Direct and open communication, personal confrontation and feedback, and an in-depth analysis of the way things are and the client's leadership style, which may be unwittingly maintaining the status quo, may be far more than the client bargained for. Not all these events may occur, but the potential is there. If the client's level of motivation is questionable, he or she may want to keep things superficial, with little risk taking and a tendancy to back off at the first barrier to be hurdled. Developing a realistic and clear contract with the consultant, in which potential problems, options, benefits, and mode of operation are spelled out (as much as possible), is an important initial phase of the OD effort.

Before contacting a consultant, it will be helpful to managers to find out as much as possible about the type of consultation they need for the problems they want to address. This information can be gathered through reading a book like this one, which gives an overview of OD and OD consultation; by talking to other managers or colleagues, particularly those who have used consultants; and by attending workshops like the NTL's "Introduction to OD." Managers can also conduct initial surveys in their departments, through either questionnaires or interviews, to check out their perceptions of what is needed or not needed. Getting some clarity on their department's needs will enable them to assess more adequately the type of help they need from a consultant. Once this preconsultant preparation is completed, managers will know how to use a consultant.

What do I have to do to be an
OD consultant for the organization?

The question refers to being an internal organizational consultant, as opposed to an external consultant. Most of what will be addressed, however, will apply to both internal and prospective external consultants.

In many OD programs, people emerge who are interested in, and excited by, the work and role of a change agent. These people, often on their own initiative, may begin to develop skills in the areas of training, consultation, and OD. In this way, external consultants can gradually reduce their consultation time to the organization as the internal consultants pick up more of the responsibility for the OD program. Pairing with external OD consultants, as described earlier, is one excellent way of learning to be a consultant. Prospective internal consultants can be sponsored by their organization to obtain training in OD from organizations such as the NTL Institute for Applied Behavioral Science. Although the NTL Institute does not certify consultants, it has had more impact on the field than any other institution through its workshops, publications, and journal *(Journal of Applied Behavioral Science)* and through its history and association with OD and OD consultants. Other associations to which one may apply for membership are the OD Division of the American Society for Training and Development, in Madison, Wisconsin; the Academy of Management Division of OD, in Norman, Oklahoma; and the OD Network, formerly associated with the NTL Institute, in Alexandria, Virginia. A good start is to attend a basic human interaction workshop in which one is personally involved in a developing T-group that examines its own group process, gives feedback to group members about their behavior and leadership style, and receives conceptual support to clarify ongoing group events. Hanson and Lubin (1987) presented a model for self-development in which trainers and consultants can set their own personal and professional goals and monitor their own progress along a variety of dimensions (see Appendix C of this book). In terms of general learning goals for potential internal consultants, it pays to learn as much as possible about the culture in which one works, the values of one's internal "clients" (other members of one's organization), and organization members' perceptions of their roles, their goals and means of accomplishing them, and how their efforts affect the mission of the organization.

We would like to insert a caveat here. In the course of learning to be a consultant, learners are exposed to a wide variety of structured exercises and styles of group leadership. Regardless of how attractive some of these techniques are, consultants must always ask themselves, "Is this exercise appropriate or relevant to the learning goals of this client or to the situation being addressed, or is it just one of my favorite interventions?" Remember, it is the client's needs that should be met, not the consultant's.

We have suggested some routes through which potential consultants can gain conceptual and experiential knowledge about OD consultation, philosophy, theory, and technology. Other, personal attributes that are not learned as easily, if at all, are critical for effective consultation relationships. It helps if the consultant has a high tolerance for ambiguity and frustration; the ability to influence others and confront difficult situations; an openness to being influenced and hearing feedback; the ability to listen and check for understanding; a willingness to take risks and to experiment with alternative ways of doing things in the face of traditional norms and procedures even if there is a potential danger of losing the contract; a capacity to support and nurture others; the sensitivity to recognize his or her own feelings and attitudes; the ability to maintain a sense of humor, particularly when the going gets rough; and a willingness to settle for small, short-term successes in order to obtain higher long-term payoffs.

How do I handle resistance to change, to being influenced, to being helped, and to participating in the program?

Many managers have asked questions concerning clients' not buying into an OD program—for example, "What if one or a few members do not want to participate?" "Suppose the manager rejects the philosophy underlying OD?" "Several members are ready to participate, others are hanging back; what do I do?" How do we know when resisting the program is "resistance" or the expression of a legitimate concern? This question touches some of the consultants' anxieties about their own competence, and will be responded to in some detail.

Resistance of clients is part of the reality that consultants have to address; it is also one of the most disconcerting aspects of OD. We have addressed resistance to change to some extent in Chapter 4. Some consultants may aggress against the resistance and find that their confrontative stance only increases the defensiveness of the client. Others are able to accept the resistance as part of their work and do not take it personally. The resistance is against what the client perceives the consultant as asking him or her to do, not against the consultant per se. Remember, clients are being asked to confront a difficult reality that they have been avoiding, to make a difficult choice, or to take an unpopular action (Block, 1981, p. 120). Resistance, it must also be remembered, is an indirect expression of some underlying anxieties. We must not lose sight of the fact that we are dealing with human beings. Calling them managers, employees, consultants, and clients tends to obscure this fact. Human beings have ways of handling threats to their survival, personal and psychological safety, and self-esteem that may be thoroughly ingrained, habitual, and difficult to change. On the organizational level, resistance to change produces routines that are habitually used to protect the organization from having its vulnerabilities exposed. Argyris (1993) defined "an *organizational defensive routine* as any policy or action that inhibits individuals, groups, intergroups and organizations from experiencing embarrassment or threat and, at the same time, prevents the actors from identifying and reducing the causes of embarrassment or threat. Organizational defensive routines are antilearning and overprotective" (p. 15). For an additional easy-to-read exploration of these concepts, see Argyris (1990).

In summary, we cannot change other people. We can, however, create conditions that make change less threatening and in which others may choose to change. The responsibility for change lies in the client.

Resistance to change is an emotional response to any change in the status quo, which is perceived (realistically or unrealistically) as more comfortable and secure than the unknown quality of something different. Some changes may be perceived as so threatening that groups or individuals may engage in resistant behavior that appears to be unproductive at best and self-destructive at worst. It is important to recognize that resistance is not an isolated phenomenon but is embedded in family, group, or cultural norms that may be perceived as in danger of being violated by a change program. It is therefore important to accept resistance and the feelings behind it as legitimate, and to work with it from there. Again, to meet resistance with antagonism and pressure to change will increase the resistance and may foster a counterdependent attitude. Change always involves some conflict or stress. Conflict is neither good nor bad; it is part of everyday life. The ways in which the conflict or stress is managed or resolved, however, can be critical to the effectiveness of any attempt to solve problems or engage in a change program (Hanson, 1981, pp. 34-35). Some of the ways in which resistance manifests itself are:

1. Rebelling, attacking, or ridiculing the program and/or the consultant, being abusive or unreachable, refusing to participate in, or comply with, program activities.

2. Frequently being tardy or absent, leaving early, going in and out during sessions, or showing up at the wrong place or wrong time.

3. Acting confused or unaware of what's going on, blocking, misunderstanding, not getting the point.

4. Jumping from topic to topic, repeatedly being off target, introducing irrelevant topics or discussions, staying in the abstract, keeping things general rather than specific, intellectualizing, beating about the bush, talking *about* rather than *to* other people, not looking at the person to whom one is talking, being excessively polite or indirect rather than straightforward and direct, using excessive jargon or stereotyped language, or staying in the future or past when the present is more relevant.

5. Appearing not to see things as important or not to take them seriously, laughing off what others say, kidding around or using humor excessively, belittling others, or keeping others at a distance, not allowing close contact.

6. Not being in touch with or owning one's own feelings, being unaware of one's body and bodily sensations, experiencing no or mild emotions (as a substitute for strong feelings), frequently being tired or sleepy during sessions, not being able to sit still, having headaches, backaches, or dizziness. (Hanson, 1981, pp. 35-36)

The above forms of resistance apply more to employees already involved in an OD program. Many are also applicable to managers. The following behaviors apply more to the "reluctant" client at the front end of a project. They are taken mainly from Block (1981, pp. 114-120):

1. Asking for or giving too much detail, involving minute details or details irrelevant to issues.

2. Time availability—Manager or client always too busy, keeps consultant on a string, allows too many interruptions (e.g., phone calls, checking with secretary).

3. Accusing consultant of being impractical or academic, of not living in the real world with real problems. The intensity of the client is the key to indicate presence of resistance.

4. Confusion—After consultant explains two or three times, the client is still confused. Client blocks him- or herself from hearing and understanding.

5. Intellectualizing—Client explores theory after theory of why things are as they are. This strategy takes the pain out of the situation.

6. Silence—The client gives very little or no response, assumes a very passive role, blocks his or her own reaction.

7. Moralizing—Problems are created by others (e.g., "those people," "they need to understand," "shoulds," implying how things ought to be). Reflects a position of superiority. "They don't understand" really means "They don't agree."

8. Flight into health—As the consultant gets closer to the time of starting, the client no longer has the problem. Somehow it has solved itself.

9. Pressing for solutions—Before there is a full understanding of the problem, the client pushes for a solution. This strategy keeps the client dependent on the consultant to solve the problem. It may also "suck in" a consultant who is eager to please.

Any change programs that threaten to undermine the control needs of clients (loss of power to manage situation and those involved in it) or expose their vulnerabilities (loss of self-esteem and sense of competency) will be met with resistance. Part of the solution is to help clients to express their underlying concerns directly rather than indirectly through resistance maneuvers. The direct expression of underlying concerns is not resistance. The client is stating what is true for him or her.

What are some personal guidelines for consultants?

Below are a few personal characteristics that are important for a consultant-client relationship. They can also apply to any relationship in which openness, clarity, and integrity are key ingredients.

Authenticity. It is important to be as open and honest as possible. Do not agree or disagree merely to please or antagonize clients. Openness elicits openness. Hiding behaviors such as feelings, private agendas, and control needs is usually sensed by the other person and elicits closedness and distrust.

Nonjudgmental Attitude. When consulting, it is usually not helpful to make or pass judgments on clients such as telling them they are right or wrong, good or bad, fair or unfair. Not only does this take away the responsibility of clients to assess the effectiveness or ineffectiveness of their own behavior, but it implies imposing standards (one's own) on others. For most of us, judgments arise almost automatically; when this is happening, own it for what it is, then phrase your question or reaction in a way that enables clients to make the assessment (not judgment) about their own behavior.

Congruence. Communication is frequently confusing when consultants' behavior is not congruent with their feelings (e.g., smiling when they are angry, expressing anger or affection when they really do not feel it). The person on the receiving end may not know which behaviors to respond to (e.g., the tone of voice or the content of what is being said) and feel in a double-bind situation. Consequently, instead of being focused on the issue to be resolved, their energy is drained by their trying to figure out what consultants are really communicating. A good match between feelings and behavior allows both consultant and client to invest their energies in the problem-solving process.

Listening. Listening is an active process. It requires attending to what the other person is communicating—not only the content of what is being communicated but the way it is being communicated. Listening involves such things as tone of voice, inflection, the feelings behind the voice, brief versus rambling exposition, and directness versus indirectness, as well as the words themselves. The focus of attention should be on the client, not on the consultant and his or her own thoughts (e.g., thoughts about how he or she is going to respond to the client).

Seeing. Seeing the client increases the quality of the contact and the clarity of what is being communicated. Seeing is actively attending and is not a passive process. It involves noticing such things as facial expressions, use of hands and body movements, body positions, eye contact, and other visual cues that enrich the communication process. Again, the focus of attention is external (on the other person), not internal (on oneself).

Facilitating. One of the primary functions of consultants is to help clients identify and explore their own feelings, perceptions, attitudes, and behaviors that bear on the situation, in reference to themselves, to others, and to the situation. Questions should be geared toward clarification of these issues, enabling clients to assess how they handle the problem or implement the goal. Giving advice, offering solutions, or guessing the motivations of others in the client's world as they relate to the problem not only takes away the responsibility of clients to work their own issues but turns the consultation process into a guessing game.

In the final analysis, what type of consultant, manager, or person do you want to be—one who plays it close to the vest or one who is relatively unguarded and open? Remember, openness elicits openness in others, closedness elicits closed and guarded responses from others.

OD Evaluation

Who benefits from an OD effort?
In my department? In my organization?

Who benefits from an OD program can best be answered by those directly involved, particularly the client(s) and the consultant. If an OD program is effective, it can benefit not only the individual manager, but those people with whom he or she has contact, such as supervisors, subordinates, the organizational community, and other managers. If an effective OD program means a climate of openness and sharing, a revitalization of people within the organizational community, greater job satisfaction and commitment to departmental or organizational goals, and a greater sense of responsibility and ownership among employees, then everyone benefits. In a very real sense, the entire organization and all the people in it are the "clients" of an effective OD effort. As the OD program affects and involves adjacent work units and departments, its effects spread and permeate the total organization.

The organization can benefit to the extent that the individual departments clarify or redefine their role and mission and develop a method for translating that mission into effective action within the organizational structure. For example, managers of these departments may take on the behavioral science function within the organization, becoming internal consultants to their own work units and to the whole system.

To determine who benefits and how much, the consultant and the client can decide on what constitutes "benefit," "satisfaction," or "commitment" and develop measures or questionnaires to make the feelings, attitudes, and perceptions of the members explicit. Sometimes a simple rating scale can be used to collect this data. Sample instruments are discussed in the questions below and appear in Appendix A.

What are signs that OD is working or not working in my organization?

These signs are described in Chapter 4. The items can be converted into criterion measures for program outcomes. For example, "shared decision making, more involvement and commitment to decisions made, and quicker implementation" represents one of the signs, but can be divided into several scaled questions:

- Do you share in the decisions made in your work unit?
- How involved do you feel in the decisions your team makes?
- How committed do you feel to the decisions in your department?
- How quickly are these decisions put into action?

Under each question would be a scale running from low to high on the item addressed—for example, (1) *low commitment* to (7) *high commitment.* Employees would circle the number that best reflected the degree of their commitment. The procedure would be repeated for the other items. The consultant and client could select those signs to be converted and decide what level of ratings constituted a criterion for success. A more detailed discussion appears in later in this chapter.

How can we evaluate our own OD program in our department/organization? How can we make sure it will have practical, measurable effects? How do we measure and evaluate the outcome?

These questions are essentially asking the same thing. Because program evaluation is a critical part of any OD effort, we will respond in some detail.

Systematic program evaluation has been much needed but often avoided by both the OD consultant and the manager. When evaluation does take place, it is usually informal—a verbal response from managers to the question "How are we doing?" or a tally of degrees of satisfaction and relevancy with comments and/or a few open-ended questions. Part of the problem is, first, that program evaluation is seen as requiring a high degree of sophistication in statistical design. Second, it is often confused with research and experimental design, putting it beyond the realm of the manager's competence. Third, it is difficult to nail down specific measurable items that will reflect the goals or objectives of the OD effort. Fourth, by-products of OD programs are often hard to identify or predict and are frequently overlooked in an evaluation program (e.g., some managers develop competency in OD technology). Last, it is difficult to predict when the results of an OD program will emerge with sufficient visibility and clarity so that they can be measured. Ongoing follow-up evaluation and feedback of results are OD interventions in themselves.

Because of the importance of program evaluation, the response to this question will shift to a more "how-to" focus touching some of the highlights of the process of evaluation. There are several approaches to evaluating the OD program in your department or organization; these may or may not require consultation from a consultant who has expertise in the area of program evaluation. Any evaluation program, however, needs to be worked out by the manager or supervisor involved in the project and his or her team. The manager and the team need to spell out the goals of the program and determine along what dimensions they want to measure change (e.g., individual and team behaviors, work performance and productivity, and those criteria listed in Chapter 4). These goals should be described in such a way that movement toward or away from the objective can be measured. Once these dimensions are defined, the manager and his or her team need to assess where the department is currently functioning along these dimensions, where they would like it to be, and how they can tell when the objectives or goals have been achieved.

Program evaluation does not have to be a highly complicated project, with all types of statistical procedures and tests of significance. Measures of goal achievement can be very simple (e.g., 75% of those involved in the program say, "Yes, we have reached our objective"). Once the manager and his team have decided upon the criterion level of success, along the dimensions selected as appropriately describing departmental goals (the most difficult part of program evaluation and thus the most frequently avoided), the actual data collection can be turned over to a clerk. The criteria of success provide a standard of comparison against which the department can measure its current functioning and the distance it needs to move to achieve its goals. It is important to emphasize that the periodic diagnostic evaluations be fed back to the team and used for critiquing the unit's performance, continued goal setting, action planning, and implementation.

Ideally, evaluation should begin before the OD program is implemented. At this time the goals of the program are stated in a way that they can be assessed and a diagnostic survey is taken that indicates where the organization/ department is now and where members would like it to be. This diagnosis, of course, is based on the dimensions chosen to reflect these goals (e.g., more adequate planning, quicker implementation of decisions, higher productivity, job satisfaction). For example, one goal of a team-building effort may be better communication. This goal is still too broad and needs to be more specific to measure. The manager and work team members may decide that "participation" and "being listened to" are two of the dimensions under communication that they wish to assess. The goal statements may appear as scales on which team members check their own performance or how they perceive the team functioning. Using a Likert-type format, we have:

Circle the appropriate numbers related to how you see your work situation *now* and how you *would like it to be.*

1. COMMUNICATION

a. The level of my participation at team meetings is:

	Very low			Average		Very high	
Now	1	2	3	4	5	6	7
Would like	1	2	3	4	5	6	7

b. I feel that my contributions are listened to and considered in this department:

	Not at all			Half the time		All the time	
Now	1	2	3	4	5	6	7
Would like	1	2	3	4	5	6	7

Once a diagnostic picture is available of how team members see the situation now and how they would like it to be, the manager and the team need to determine the criteria that constitute goal achievement (i.e., "How can we tell when we are where we want to be?"). Under "participation," they may choose, as a criterion of success, a minimum score of 4 or 5 checked by *all* team members. A score of 7 might not be desirable because it might indicate that everyone is talking and no one is listening. On the "listening" scale, however, a score of 7 might be desirable, and the criterion of success could be set at 5 to 7 for all team members. Criterion setting is a rational process based upon the nature of the situation and the people involved and may differ from one dimension to another. Once these criteria have been achieved, work on these dimensions needs to be ongoing in order to maintain the criterion level of success. Goal achievement is not a one-shot event. It is very easy for organizations, departments, or work teams to slip back into old, ineffective patterns of behavior. In addition, periodic diagnostic assessments of where the unit is provide feedback data for the team or department to critique itself and to solve its internal problems. This data collection and feedback to the managers and employees is the essence of action research.

Consultants also have numerous diagnostic instruments to get at work climate, motivation, supervisor/subordinate relations, and so forth. Unobtrusive measures such as personnel files, profit and loss statements, waste, and meeting target dates may also be identified, with the consultant's help, as appropriate measures of goal achievement or by-products of OD programs. A critical dimension of the total quality programs is the use of statistical tools to identify problems and measure progress (see Chapter 6). Instruments can also be tailored to fit specific situations.

Another approach to OD program evaluation is to compare your department or work team with other similar organizational units that do not have an OD program. Again, measurements reflecting the current status of the units need to be taken before the program begins. These measures will indicate to what extent the units are comparable to begin with and whether they can be used for comparison purposes. The managers of those departments involved need to decide, in any event, which units are comparable. This comparison of two departments is risky and requires some sensitivity. If Department A shows up as more effective and productive than Department B, Department B may feel threatened and resent Department A. On the other hand, Department B may perceive the superior performance of Department A as an incentive to do better. Again, the manager and his or her team determine the criterion measures of success—that is, how much change must occur in one department over another before the criterion of success will be considered to have been achieved.

After a program has begun, it is somewhat more difficult to obtain a before-and-after measure of change. Departmental employees or team members may rate retrospectively (e.g., how things were before the OD program began, how things are now, and how they would like things to be). This retrospective evaluation is not as satisfactory as the before-and-after ratings. In any event, the same procedures are followed for establishing goal statements in measurable form, deciding criterion levels of success, and setting target dates for periodic assessment. It is important to reemphasize that the data collected from the team members reflecting their perceptions of team functioning must be fed back to the team. This data feedback enables the team to identify trouble spots, modify its operations, and implement action steps toward resolving its problems and achieving its goals.

The term *diagnosis* appears frequently in the literature. How do I go about diagnosing my team, my department? How do I get started?

Diagnosis is a search for "what is going on now in my team or in my department." When things are not going right, or something is blocking us from functioning more effectively, we need to examine how the team is currently functioning. We can do this in a variety of ways. The first is direct observation. The consultant can arrange to observe the client or client group as it goes about its daily routines. This includes meeting initially with the client, sitting in on staff conferences and other work meetings, and observing interactions between manager and employees and among employees. In this way, the consultant can get an impression of the work climate (e.g., happy, tense, formal, informal), how business is conducted, and how people relate to each other. This in vivo survey will also give the consultant ideas to incorporate into a more objective data collection design. The consultant will have to be unobtrusive in his or her observer role. It is probably best if the consultant is introduced to the employees and the nature of his or her presence explained.

The second method of diagnosis is individual and group interviews. The consultant will probably interview key individuals to get their individual perspective of "how things are"; the organization's mission, the department's mission, and how the two are related; and their own relation to the mission and to other members. A structured interview form can be used to provide consistency across interviews. Open-ended comments can be solicited after the structured part is completed. Avoid asking questions in a way that elicits "yes" or "no" responses. The questions should serve as a stimulus to discuss feelings and areas of activities and concerns. In one-on-one interviews, the goal is free and open discussion of issues rather than the brevity that one would seek from mailed questionnaires. See Appendix A for a sample structured interview.

If many people must be interviewed (e.g., employees), the consultant may conduct these sessions in small groups of 8 to 12 individuals. Again, the consultant may want to use a structured form that contains the questions from which he or she collects information. These sessions have an additional payoff for the consultant and the group. First, the consultant can get an idea of how much agreement or disagreement there is among the perceptions of the employees as to the mission of the organization, the mission of their department, and their own roles. Second, the group session can be an educational experience for the group members. They can compare their individual perspectives with other group members, discuss the differences and similarities, and obtain greater clarity about the organizational and departmental operations and their contribution to the mission.

Both of these types of interviews provide data for further observations and for the construction of survey instruments, questionnaires, and rating scales. A reminder: At some point during the diagnostic process, the data should be fed back to the organizational members. When this data feedback occurs should be decided upon by both the consultant and the client or manager.

A third method of diagnosis is questionnaires, rating scales, and other survey instruments. *Questionnaires* are usually used when there are many people to be surveyed. They may be distributed in a large-group session or mailed to the target population. When practical, it is better, for a large group (e.g., 50-100 or more people), to administer questionnaires directly than to mail them out. There is a better chance of getting a large return, and returns are immediate. Also, participants can ask for clarification on any unclear items. Furthermore, the lower percentage of mailed returns (50% is usually high) may represent a biased sample (e.g., of members who are more highly motivated). Finally, the mail-out questionnaire is a more impersonal way of collecting data and may receive indifferent attention by less conscientious recipients. A better rate of return can be expected when the questionnaire is short, the questions are brief and uncomplicated, and a short response is requested.

Individual, group, and organizational behavior *rating scales* can follow some of the same suggestions noted above. Several diagnostic instruments on the market may provide an adequate diagnosis, but may not contain some of the issues consultants and clients wish to explore for their own organization. For more comprehensive assessment, behavioral rating scales can be created from the information collected during interviews such as those described above and from issues or behaviors the consultant and client want to explore.

The following material offers guidelines for creating scales. The two scales illustrated below will serve as a model for discussion.

Participation: My level of participation at team meetings is:

Very low					Very high	
1	2	3	4	5	6	7

Participation:

One or two people dominate, others are silent or respond minimally.					All team members actively participate as the need arises.	
1	2	3	4	5	6	7

Focus of Item: Perception of Self Versus Team. In the first scale, the participants will be rating their perception of the level of their own participation. When these ratings are accumulated, we will get an average rating based on self-perceptions. Self-perceptions cannot be labeled right or wrong; they are true for the individual. The second scale represents participants' perceptions of the team—other people's behavior. Again, a perception cannot be labeled right or wrong; it can, however, be compared with other people's perceptions. In comparisons of the two points of view, interesting information may emerge: For example, participants may rate themselves as low on participation level (Scale 1), but their average rating of the team level of participation (Scale 2) may be high.

Number of Points on a Scale. The above scales have 7 points. This number may or may not be acceptable for what consultants and clients have in mind. Too many points (9 or 10) may give the impression that what is being measured is clear, but complex enough to warrant minute gradations of discrimination. Because most ratings are subjective and on behaviors that are not highly defined, too many points give a false impression. On the other hand, too few points do not allow for sufficient discrimination to be meaningful. Two few points are also less desirable to deal with statistically. What does an average of 2 mean on a 3-point scale? Some questions, however, require a yes or no answer; these are converted to a "1" or "2" response for purposes of analysis.

Contamination of Items. Contamination can occur in at least two ways:
1. When more than one dimension is contained in the stem (e.g., "group members' participation *and* involvement"). Some group members may not participate (talk) very much but feel very involved. Others may participate a lot but feel very little involvement. This item should be written as two separate scales.

2. When the content of the scale is mixed with the scale itself, (e.g., "How *highly* involved are participants?" as opposed to "How involved are participants?"). In the first question, *highly* really represents an end point on the scale. To answer "low" would appear contradictory. The second question allows the rater to select the point on the scale that best represents his or her judgment without being influenced by the word *highly*.

The Use of Words That Represent a Continuum. If the data are going to be treated statistically, the use of words that can be graded on a continuum is more desirable (e.g., *high control → moderate control → low control*). Discrete items are not graded and thus not amenable to computing averages. They can, however, be used in counting individuals who "circled" certain words: For example, words to describe group climate (e.g., *tense, happy, sluggish*). Here the results will show, not average ratings on an item, but only how many individuals checked which word—for example, *tense* (5), *happy* (2), *sluggish* (6). This information is useful for discussion but has limitations for research evaluations. These words, however, can be converted to scales.

Many instruments are developed from theories of personal, group, and organizational behavior, such as those on leadership styles (Blake & Mouton, 1964); interpersonal needs (Leary, 1957; Schutz, 1978); group role behavior (Bales, 1970; Bass, 1962); orienting functions (Myers-Briggs Type Indicator [MBTI]—Keirsey & Bates, 1984; Kroeger & Thuesen, 1988; Myers, 1980); Systems 4 Management Survey Feedback—Likert, 1967; Likert & Likert, 1976). For review and assessment of instruments measuring a variety of behaviors in various settings, see Lake, Miles and Earle (1973) and Pfeiffer, Heslin, and Jones (1976).

Sample Diagnostic Instruments

Team and Organization Diagnosis

Below are sample items from two diagnostic instruments that readers can complete for their own work units or organizations to get a feel for how these instruments are used. They are primarily "sensing" instruments to give the manager or team leader information about his or her own work unit and organization. They are not intended to generate comparison data for other organizations. The first instrument, "How I See My Organization," is concerned with the organization as a whole. The items on the second instrument, "How I See My Work Unit or Team," overlap the first instrument but are more geared toward a group setting. When employees complete these instruments, tallies can be made or averages computed for each item so that managers and team members can see how their perceptions of the organization or work team compare with one another. A profile can be constructed by connecting the average scores on each item for the "now" ratings. It is important to keep the tallies along with the average points so that one can see the spread of ratings: the highs and lows, where scores tend to accumulate, and how widely scores are distributed. The same procedure can be followed for the "would like" ratings. Once the profiles are drawn, discrepancies between the "now" and "would like" ratings for each item can be compared. The largest discrepancies may provide a starting point for managers and their team to set goals and begin a program change. Managers and their team may also select particular items as OD goals and designate the "would like" ratings as indicators of goal achievement.

Readers may draw their own profile by connecting, vertically, the points they have checked on each item. When you look at your profile, you will probably begin to think about the things in your work unit that influenced your ratings. Ask a colleague to complete the same scale and discuss the similarities with and differences from your own ratings. This discussion may generate new information that you have not previously considered and clarify or put in a different light old issues that have been vague or taken for granted. The process you and your colleague went through of sharing perceptions of your work team or department is one of the initial steps in organization development.

Diagnosing Organizational Effectiveness

Included are sample items from each of the original instruments (Hanson & Burke, 1977). Each form contains 23 items.

Form A: How I See the Organization

In this section you will be considering how you view the *organization as a whole.* In rating each item, first circle the number on the scale that most closely approximates the way you see the total organization functioning NOW. Then rate the item again, this time circling the number that best describes how you WOULD LIKE to see the total organization functioning.

Remember, you are to rate the items in terms of *your* view of the total organization.

Form B: How I See My Work Unit or Team

In this section, you will be considering how you view your *particular work unit or team* within the organization. In making these ratings, you will be considering some of the same or similar items that you have rated before, as well as some new items. This time, however, you will be focusing on the organizational work unit in which you do all or most of your work.

In rating each item, first circle the number on the scale that most closely approximates the way you see your work unit or team functioning NOW. Then rate the item again, this time circling the number that best describes how you WOULD LIKE to see your work unit or team functioning.

Remember, this time you are to rate the items in terms of *your* view of your work unit or team.

FORM A: HOW I SEE MY ORGANIZATION

1. Goal setting:

Now	1	2	3	4	5	6	7
Would like	1	2	3	4	5	6	7

Goals are set at top levels & imposed downward.

Organizational units participate in setting goals & share ownership of them.

2. Communication style:

Now	1	2	3	4	5	6	7
Would like	1	2	3	4	5	6	7

Communication is guarded, cautious, closed; censored communication flow.

Straightforward, free & open, uncensored.

3. Listening to others:

Now	1	2	3	4	5	6	7
Would like	1	2	3	4	5	6	7

Individuals rarely take time to stop & listen to others. Preoccupied, do not attend to what is being said, passive.

Individuals take time to hear others out, check for understanding what is being said, are attentive & actively listen.

4. Feedback:

Now	1	2	3	4	5	6	7
Would like	1	2	3	4	5	6	7

Employees & work units are rarely told how they are doing or where they stand, no sharing of effectiveness data.

Employees & work units always told how they are doing & where they stand, full sharing of effectiveness data.

5. Communication in organization:

Now	1	2	3	4	5	6	7
Would like	1	2	3	4	5	6	7

Lines & origins of communications are

Lines & origins of communication are

unclear, rumors abound,
information distrusted
or tardy or lost.

clear, people feel
fully informed & up
to date, trust
information, rumors
minimal.

6. Decision making:

Now	1	2	3	4	5	6	7
Would like	1	2	3	4	5	6	7

Made mostly at top
level and handed down.

All levels involved
in making decisions
where appropriate.

7. Leadership:

Now	1	2	3	4	5	6	7
Would like	1	2	3	4	5	6	7

Authority-centered
by position and title.

Team-centered by
resources & nature
of task.

8. Handling of conflict:

Now	1	2	3	4	5	6	7
Would like	1	2	3	4	5	6	7

Little or no tolerance
for disagreements or
different points of view,
employees expected to
follow "party line."

High tolerance for
disagreement, diff-
erences accepted &
considered with
wide latitude,
encouraged when
possible.

9. Problem solving:

Now	1	2	3	4	5	6	7
Would like	1	2	3	4	5	6	7

Solutions to problems
jumped to prematurely
with little or no diagnosis
& planning.

Solutions to
problems proposed
& planned after full
diagnosis of
problem & all the
forces affecting it.

10. Organizational structure:

Now	1	2	3	4	5	6	7
Would like	1	2	3	4	5	6	7

Operates bureaucratically,
bogged down by hierarchy,

Operates fluidly &
organically, pro-

procedures, policies, & inflexible rules.

cedures, policies, & rules facilitate movement & flexibility.

11. Work unit operations:

Now	1	2	3	4	5	6	7
Would like	1	2	3	4	5	6	7

No clear-cut system for doing things, establishing priorities, setting goals; policies vague & ill defined.

System is clear-cut, goals & procedures are known to every-one; policies clear & understood.

12. Role definition:

Now	1	2	3	4	5	6	7
Would like	1	2	3	4	5	6	7

Work roles & functions of members from different departments are confused & needlessly overlap, much duplication of effort.

Work roles & functions of different departments & work unit members are clear; overlapping & duplication are minimal.

13. Utilization of employees' resources:

Now	1	2	3	4	5	6	7
Would like	1	2	3	4	5	6	7

Talents, skills, experience, & ideas of employees not identified, sought, or acknowledged.

Talents, skills, experience, & ideas identified & fully utilized where & when appropriate.

14. Creativity:

Now	1	2	3	4	5	6	7
Would like	1	2	3	4	5	6	7

Innovation is discouraged, routine ways not questioned, rule book & uniform procedures followed.

There is a willing-ness to try new ways of doing things, questioning old ways, innovation is encouraged.

FORM B: HOW I SEE MY WORK UNIT OR TEAM

1. Goal setting:

Now	1	2	3	4	5	6	7
Would like	1	2	3	4	5	6	7

Team or work unit goals are set for us from above.

Goals set by team, emerging through team interaction and agreement.

2. Participation:

Now	1	2	3	4	5	6	7
Would like	1	2	3	4	5	6	7

One or two people dominate, others silent or respond minimally.

All team members actively participate as the need arises.

3. Listening:

Now	1	2	3	4	5	6	7
Would like	1	2	3	4	5	6	7

Team members are cut off or interrupted, little or no attending.

Team members hear each other out before moving on to others, very attentive.

4. Feedback:

Now	1	2	3	4	5	6	7
Would like	1	2	3	4	5	6	7

Little or no sharing about how well members are working together or how they affect team or work unit effectiveness.

Members ask for & give feedback freely, share how they stand with each other & how well they are contributing to team or work unit effectiveness.

5. Communication on work unit:

Now	1	2	3	4	5	6	7
Would like	1	2	3	4	5	6	7

Lines of communication are unclear, information tardy or lost.

Lines of communication are clear, people feel fully informed & up to date.

6. Decision making:

Now	1	2	3	4	5	6	7
Would like	1	2	3	4	5	6	7

Influential few push through decisions made by unit manager or supervisor.

All members are encouraged to participate in decision, full agreement of team sought.

7. Leadership:

Now	1	2	3	4	5	6	7
Would like	1	2	3	4	5	6	7

Much depending on one or two members to get things done, others "wait & see" without much involvement.

Leadership distributed & shared among members, individuals contribute when their resources are needed.

8. Handling team conflicts:

Now	1	2	3	4	5	6	7
Would like	1	2	3	4	5	6	7

No tolerance for expression of negative feelings or confrontation, conflicts "swept under the rug."

Negative feelings & tension shared & confronted within team, conflict seen as potential source of creative team effort.

9. Problem solving:

Now	1	2	3	4	5	6	7
Would like	1	2	3	4	5	6	7

Little or no attempt to look at team issues or problems, no real diagnosis of forces affecting work unit functioning.

Team diagnoses problems or team issues and critiques its own effectiveness and all the forces affecting team functioning.

10. Work unit structure:

Now	1	2	3	4	5	6	7
Would like	1	2	3	4	5	6	7

Work unit operates mechanically, bogged down by procedures, agendas, hierarchy, and inflexible rules.

Procedures, agendas, lines of authority, & norms are fluid, allowing for maximum flexibility within the team.

11. Work unit operations:

Now	1	2	3	4	5	6	7
Would like	1	2	3	4	5	6	7

No clear-cut system for doing things, establishing priorities, or setting policies.

The system here is clear-cut, policies and procedures are known to everyone.

12. Role definition:

Now	1	2	3	4	5	6	7
Would like	1	2	3	4	5	6	7

Work roles & functions of work unit members are confused & needlessly overlap.

Work roles & function of work unit members are clear; overlapping & duplication are minimal.

13. Utilizing resources of team members:

Now	1	2	3	4	5	6	7
Would like	1	2	3	4	5	6	7

Talents, skills, & experience of team members not identified, sought out, or given recognition.

Talents, skills, & experience of team members are fully identified, recognized, & utilized whenever appropriate.

14. Creativity:

Now	1	2	3	4	5	6	7
Would like	1	2	3	4	5	6	7

Little or no risk taking or experimenting with new ideas or ways of doing things.

Trying new ways & ideas is encouraged, risk taking is supported.

Group Rating Scale

The scale below is another sensing device that can be used in a group or team setting. It is intended to ascertain the current status of the dynamics of the group or team as it is perceived by its members. Each group member circles the number on each scale that best describes his or her perception of where the group is currently functioning on that dimension. After the group members have completed their ratings, it is helpful if the tallies (all group members' ratings) are plotted on a chart of the 12 items. In this way, the group members have a picture of the total number of tallies for each item and their distribution on the scales. Members can now see where the tallies are concentrated or widely dispersed on the scales. It is important that group members discuss the basis for their ratings. These discussions generate a considerable amount of information, not previously evident, about group members' perceptions of the group's present functioning. These data can then be used to set up goals for improving the group's effectiveness. Averages for each scale can be computed and plotted over time for repeated administrations.

This intervention has several benefits:

- It objectifies individual perceptions by grouping them with other team members' perceptions and creating a more comprehensive analysis of the team's functioning.
- It enables individual team members to compare their individual perceptions with other group members' perceptions and to see to what extent they are in line with, or deviate from, the norm.
- It focuses the attention of the group on their here-and-now functioning.
- It provides a basis for future goal setting.

GROUP RATING SCALE

Rate your group on each scale by circling the number that best describes where your group is now. Place tallies over the numbers of each scale to indicate how other group members rated the item. Discuss the group data you used for each rating and note those items that have a wide spread or tend to pile up on the middle or low end of the scales.

A. Group members keep discussions focused on activities in the group ("here and now").

1	2	3	4	5	6	7
Very infrequently					Very frequently	

B. Group members' participation in group is:

    1   2   3   4   5   6   7
    Very low, few   Very high, most
    members each   members each
    session   session

C. Group members keep the group discussions on target (avoid digression or topic jumping).

    1   2   3   4   5   6   7
    Very little   Very much

D. Group members encourage quiet members to participate ("open gates").

    1   2   3   4   5   6   7
    Very little   Very much

E. Group members are supportive of each other (e.g., make supportive statements to other group members).

    1   2   3   4   5   6   7
    Very little   Very much

F. Group members listen to and hear each other out.

    1   2   3   4   5   6   7
    Very little   Very much

G. Group members check for understanding of what is being said.

    1   2   3   4   5   6   7
    Very little   Very much

H. Group members give feedback about each other's behavior as it occurs in the group.

    1   2   3   4   5   6   7
    Very little   Very much

I. Group members ask for feedback about their own behavior.

    1   2   3   4   5   6   7
    Very little   Very much

J. Group members build on other people's feedback—add to, enlarge upon, clarify, elaborate previously expressed feedback.

    1   2   3   4   5   6   7
    Very little   Very much

K. Group members work in depth with own as well as each other's feelings.

    1   2   3   4   5   6   7
    Very infrequently   Very frequently

L. Group members feel free to express negative feelings about the group or toward each other.

1   2   3   4   5   6   7

Very little freedom   Completely free

M. The level of trust (freedom to express thoughts and feelings without fear of being hurt or hurting someone) in the group is:

1   2   3   4   5   6   7

Very low   Very high

N. Group members take full responsibility for the group's activities/discussions and direction.

1   2   3   4   5   6   7

Very few take any   Most members take
responsibility,   responsibility, not
dependent on leader   dependent on leader.

Some Behaviors to Observe During Team Meetings

The following observation guide previously appeared as "What to Look for in Groups" in Hanson (1981, pp. 164-168). The current guide has been slightly modified to apply to work team meetings. The processes described, however, are the same for both teams and groups. The guide also provides, in summary form, 10 dimensions of group process most common to group meetings. This guide has appeared in numerous publications and has been used extensively in the United States and Europe.

SOME BEHAVIORS TO OBSERVE DURING TEAM MEETINGS

In all human interactions there are two major ingredients: content and process. The first deals with subject matter or the task on which the group is working. In most interactions, the focus of attention of all persons is on the content. The second ingredient, process, is concerned with what is happening between and to group members while the group is working. Team dynamics or group process deals with such things as morale, feeling tone, atmosphere, influence, participation, styles of influence, leadership struggles, conflict, competition, and cooperation. In most interactions, very little attention is paid to process, even when it is the major cause of ineffective team action. Sensitivity to these dynamics will better enable one to diagnose team problems early and deal with them more effectively. Because these processes are present in all groups, awareness of them will enhance a person's worth to a team and enable him or her to be a more effective team participant.

Below are some observation guidelines to help one analyze the dynamics of team behavior.

Participation

One indication of involvement is verbal participation. Look for differences in the amount of participation among members.

1. Who are the high participators?
2. Who are the low participators?
3. Do you see any shift in participation (e.g., highs become quiet; lows suddenly become talkative)? Do you see any possible reason for this in the team's interaction?
4. How are the silent people treated? How is their silence interpreted? As consent? Disagreement? Disinterest? Fear?
5. Who talks to whom? Do you see any reason for this in the team's interactions?
6. Who keeps the ball rolling? Why? Do you see any reason for this in the team's interactions?

Influence

Influence and participation are not the same. Some people may speak very little, yet they capture the attention of everyone present. Others may talk a lot but are generally not listened to by other members.

7. Which members are high in influence (that is, when they talk others seem to listen)?
8. Which members are low in influence (that is, others do not listen to or follow them)? Is there any shifting in influence? Who shifts?
9. Do you see any rivalry in the team? Is there a struggle for leadership? What effect does it have on other team members?

Styles of Influence

Influence can take many forms. It can be positive or negative, it can enlist the support and cooperation of others or it can alienate them. *How* a person attempts to influence another may be the crucial factor in determining how open or closed the other will be toward being influenced. Items 10 through 13 are suggestive of four styles that frequently emerge in teams.

10. Autocratic: Does anyone attempt to impose his or her will or values on other team members or try to push them to support his or her decisions? Who evaluates or passes judgment on other team members? Do any members block action when it is not moving in the direction they desire? Who pushes to "get the members organized"?
11. Peacemaker: Who eagerly supports other members' decisions? Does anyone consistently try to prevent conflict or unpleasant feelings from being expressed

by pouring oil on the troubled waters? Is any member typically deferential toward other members—giving them power? Does any member appear to avoid giving negative feedback (i.e., levels only when he or she has positive feedback to give)?

12. Laissez-faire: Are any team members getting attention by their apparent lack of involvement? Does any member go along with team decisions without seeming to commit him- or herself one way or the other? Who seems to be withdrawn and uninvolved, does not initiate activity, participates mechanically and only in response to another member's question?

13. Participative: Does anyone try to include everyone in a team decision or discussion? Who expresses his or her feelings and opinions openly and directly without evaluating or judging others? Who appears to be open to feedback and criticisms from others? When feelings run high and tensions mount, which members attempt to deal with the conflict in a problem-solving way?

Decision-Making Procedures

Many kinds of decisions are made in work teams without consideration of the effects of these decisions on other members. Some people try to impose their own decisions on the group, whereas others want all members to participate or share in the decisions that are made.

14. Does anyone make a decision and carry it out without checking with other team members (self-authorized)? For example, does one person decide on the topic to be discussed and start right in to talk about it? What effect does this have on other members?

15. Does the team drift from topic to topic? Who topic-jumps? Do you see any reason for this in the team's interactions?

16. Who supports other members' suggestions or decisions? Does this support result in the two members' deciding the topic or activity for the team (handclasp)? How does this affect other members?

17. Is there any attempt to get all members participating in a decision (consensus)? What effect does this seem to have on the team?

19. Does anyone make any contributions that do not receive any kind of response or recognition (plop)? What effect does this have on the member?

Task Functions

These functions illustrate behaviors that are concerned with getting the job done, or accomplishing the task that the team has before it.

20. Does anyone ask for or make suggestions as to the best way to proceed or to tackle a problem?

21. Does anyone attempt to summarize what has been covered or what has been going on during the session?

22. Is there any giving or asking for facts, ideas, opinions, feelings, feedback, or searching for alternatives?

23. Who keeps team members on target—prevents topic jumping or going off on tangents?

Maintenance Functions

These functions are important to the morale of the team. They maintain good and harmonious working relationships among the members and create an atmosphere that enables each member to contribute maximally. They ensure smooth and effective teamwork.

24. Who helps others get into the discussion (gate openers)?

25. Who cuts off others or interrupts them (gate closers)?

26. How well are members getting their ideas across? Are some members preoccupied and not listening? Are there any attempts by team members to help others clarify their ideas?

27. How are ideas rejected? How do members react when their ideas are not accepted? Do members attempt to support those whose ideas are rejected?

Team Atmosphere

Something about the way a team works creates an atmosphere that in turn is revealed in a general impression. In addition, people may differ in the kind of atmosphere they like in a group. Insight can be gained into the atmosphere characteristic of a team by finding words that describe the general impressions held by team members.

28. Who seems to prefer a friendly, congenial atmosphere? Is there any attempt to suppress conflict or unpleasant feelings?

29. Who seems to prefer an atmosphere of conflict and disagreement? Do any members provoke or annoy others?

30. Do people seem involved and interested? Is the atmosphere one of work, play, satisfaction, taking flight, sluggishness?

Membership

A major concern for team members is the degree of acceptance or inclusion they feel. Different patterns of interaction may develop in the team that give clues to the degree and kind of membership.

31. Is there any subgrouping? Sometimes two or three members may consistently agree and support each other or consistently disagree and oppose one another.

32. Do some people seem to be "outside" the team? Do some members seem to be most "in"? How are those "outside" treated?

33. Do some members move in and out of the team meeting (e.g., lean forward or backward in chair or move chair in and out)? Under what conditions do they come in or move out?

Feelings

During any team discussion, feelings are frequently generated by the interactions between members. These feelings, however, are seldom talked about. Observers may have to make guesses based on tone of voice, facial expressions, gestures, and many other forms of nonverbal cues.

34. What signs of feelings do you observe in team members (anger, irritation, frustration, warmth, affection, excitement, boredom, defensiveness, competitiveness, etc.)?

35. Do you see any attempts by members to block the expression of feelings, particularly negative feelings? How is this done? Does anyone do this consistently?

Norms

Standards or ground rules may develop in a team that control the behavior of its members. Norms usually express the beliefs or desires of the majority of the members as to what behaviors *should* or *should not* take place. These norms may be clear to all members (explicit), known or sensed by only a few (implicit), or operating completely below the level of awareness of any team member. Some norms facilitate progress and some hinder it.

36. Are certain areas avoided during team meetings (e.g., underlying conflicts, talk about present feelings, discussing leader's behavior)? Who seems to reinforce this avoidance? How does he or she do it?

37. Are team members overly nice or polite to each other? Are only positive feelings expressed? Do members agree with each other too readily? What happens when members disagree?

38. Do you see norms operating about participation or the kinds of questions that are allowed (e.g., "If I talk, you must talk"; "If I tell my problems, you have to tell your problems")? Do members feel free to probe each other about their opinions and feelings? Do questions tend to be restricted to safe topics or events outside of the team?

Organizational Rating Scale—Dimensions of Effective and Ineffective Processes

The scales below focus primarily on the perceptions of the organization. The description of an effective organizational process may appear utopian. It is perhaps more a statement of direction than a state that has been achieved by any known organization.

The descriptions of the items were taken from Fordyce and Weil (1979, pp. 13-16) and converted to scales by the present authors. As with any of the scales presented in this appendix, managers can select any of the items they feel are most relevant to the issues they want to explore. They need not use all of the items on the rating scales. These scales can be treated like the other scales we have presented. Charts can be made that display the tallies and averages on each item, and criterion points (goals) ascertained through analysis and discussion. These charts represent the cumulative perceptions of the members doing the ratings and can present a picture of how members perceive their organization along the lines reflected by the items. This picture tends to objectify the ratings for the managers, who can then use the data to discuss the "experiences" of the members behind their ratings. It has been our experience that these discussions not only produce new, rich data but also create an atmosphere of sharing and openness among the members. One caveat— the managers need to impress upon the members that perceptions are neither right or wrong but are true for each individual and can only be changed by that individual when there is sufficient evidence (through discussions, feedback, interactions, etc.) to cause him or her to reevaluate the initial perception (i.e., to facilitate a change in the way the person perceives the situation).

SOME CHARACTERISTICS OF INEFFECTIVE AND EFFECTIVE ORGANIZATIONAL PROCESSES

Circle the number on each item that best approximates how you see the organization. Put tallies under each number that represents the ratings of other raters on that item. Do this for all items.

Ineffective

Effective

1. Little personal investment in organizational objectives except at top levels.

   Objectives are widely shared by the members and there is a strong & consistent flow of energy toward those objectives.

   1   2   3   4   5   6   7

2. People in the organization see things going wrong and do nothing about it. Nobody volunteers. Mistakes & problems are habitually hidden or shelved. People talk about office troubles at home or in the halls, not with those involved.

   People feel free to signal their awareness of difficulties because they expect the problems to be dealt with and they are optimistic that they can be solved.

   1   2   3   4   5   6   7

3. Extraneous factors complicate problem solving. Status & boxes on the organizational chart are more important than solving the problem. There is excessive concern with

   Problem solving is highly pragmatic. In attacking problems, people work informally and are not preoccupied with status, territory, or second-guessing

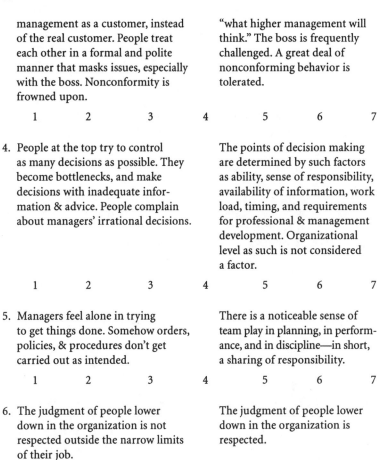

management as a customer, instead of the real customer. People treat each other in a formal and polite manner that masks issues, especially with the boss. Nonconformity is frowned upon.

"what higher management will think." The boss is frequently challenged. A great deal of nonconforming behavior is tolerated.

1   2   3   4   5   6   7

4. People at the top try to control as many decisions as possible. They become bottlenecks, and make decisions with inadequate information & advice. People complain about managers' irrational decisions.

The points of decision making are determined by such factors as ability, sense of responsibility, availability of information, work load, timing, and requirements for professional & management development. Organizational level as such is not considered a factor.

1   2   3   4   5   6   7

5. Managers feel alone in trying to get things done. Somehow orders, policies, & procedures don't get carried out as intended.

There is a noticeable sense of team play in planning, in performance, and in discipline—in short, a sharing of responsibility.

1   2   3   4   5   6   7

6. The judgment of people lower down in the organization is not respected outside the narrow limits of their job.

The judgment of people lower down in the organization is respected.

1   2   3   4   5   6   7

7. Personal needs & feelings are side issues.

The range of problems tackled includes personal needs and human relationships.

1   2   3   4   5   6   7

8. People compete when they need to collaborate. They are jealous of their area of responsibility. Seeking or accepting help is felt to be a sign of weakness. Offering help is unthought

Collaboration is freely entered into. People readily request the help of others & are willing to give in turn. Ways of helping one another are highly developed.

of. They distrust each other's motives & speak poorly of one another. The manager tolerates this.

Individuals & groups compete with one another, but they do so fairly & in the direction of a shared goal.

| 1 | 2 | 3 | 4 | 5 | 6 | 7 |

9. When there is a crisis, people withdraw or start blaming one another.

When there is a crisis, people quickly band together in work until the crisis departs.

| 1 | 2 | 3 | 4 | 5 | 6 | 7 |

10. Conflict is mostly covert & managed by office politics & other games, or there are interminable & irreconcilable arguments.

Conflicts are considered important to decision making & personal growth. They are dealt with effectively, in the open. People say what they want & expect others to do the same.

| 1 | 2 | 3 | 4 | 5 | 6 | 7 |

11. Feedback is avoided.

Joint critique of progress is routine.

| 1 | 2 | 3 | 4 | 5 | 6 | 7 |

12. Learning is difficult. People don't approach their peers to learn from them but have to learn by their own mistakes. They reject the experience of others. They get little feedback on performance & much of that is not helpful.

There is a great deal of on-the-job learning based on a willingness to give, seek, and use feedback & advice. People see themselves & others as capable of significant personal development & growth.

| 1 | 2 | 3 | 4 | 5 | 6 | 7 |

13. Relationships are contaminated by maskmanship and image building. People feel alone & lack concern for one another. There is an undercurrent of fear.

Relationships are honest. People do care about one another and do not feel alone.

| 1 | 2 | 3 | 4 | 5 | 6 | 7 |

14. People feel locked into their jobs. They feel stale & bored but

People are "turned on" and highly involved by choice. They are

constrained by the need for
security. Their behavior, for
example in staff meetings, is
listless & docile. It's not much
fun. They get their "kicks" elsewhere.

optimistic. The workplace is
important & fun. (Why not?)

| 1 | 2 | 3 | 4 | 5 | 6 | 7 |

15. The manager is a prescribing
father to the organization.

Leadership is flexible, shifting in
style and person to suit the
situation.

| 1 | 2 | 3 | 4 | 5 | 6 | 7 |

16. The manager tightly controls
small expenditures and demands
excessive justification. He allows
little freedom for making mistakes.

There is a high degree of trust
among people and a sense of
freedom & mutual responsibility.
People generally know what is
important to the organization
and what isn't.

| 1 | 2 | 3 | 4 | 5 | 6 | 7 |

17. Minimizing risk has a very high value.

Risk is accepted as a condition of
growth and change.

| 1 | 2 | 3 | 4 | 5 | 6 | 7 |

18. "One mistake and you're out."

"What can we learn from each
mistake?"

| 1 | 2 | 3 | 4 | 5 | 6 | 7 |

19. Poor performance is glossed
over or handled arbitrarily.

Poor performance is confronted
and a joint resolution is sought.

| 1 | 2 | 3 | 4 | 5 | 6 | 7 |

20. Organizational structure,
policies, & procedures encumber
the organization. People take refuge
in policies & procedures, and play
games with organization structure.

Organizational structure, procedures, and policies are fashioned
to help people get the job done
and protect the long-term health
of the organization, not to give
each bureaucrat his or her due.
They are also readily changed.

| 1 | 2 | 3 | 4 | 5 | 6 | 7 |

21. Tradition.

There is a sense of order, and yet a high rate of innovation. Old methods are questioned and often give way.

| 1 | 2 | 3 | 4 | 5 | 6 | 7 |

22. Innovation is not widespread but in the hands of a few.

The organization itself adapts swiftly to opportunities or other changes in its market-place because every pair of eyes is watching & every head is anticipating the future.

| 1 | 2 | 3 | 4 | 5 | 6 | 7 |

23. People swallow their frustra-tions. "I can do nothing. It's *their* responsibility to save the ship."

Frustrations are the call to action. "It's my/our responsibility to save the ship."

| 1 | 2 | 3 | 4 | 5 | 6 | 7 |

Structured Interview

A structured interview can be used to uncover positive and negative opinions, feelings, and perceptions about a variety of topics (e.g., clarity of the organization's mission, how decisions are made, leadership styles and their consequences, inter-departmental relations, how disagreements and mistakes are handled). The struc-tured interview differs from an unstructured interview in that it focuses on predeter-mined areas or topics as opposed to allowing the interviewee maximum latitude to bring up what he or she wants to discuss. One advantage of the structured interview is that the information can be organized and summarized more readily.

Before conducting structured interviews, the consultant or manager should have an idea in mind of the purpose of the interview and how the information is to be used—that is, the issue or issues that the manager wishes to examine. It is useful to collect, formally or informally, information that can provide guidelines for the items in the structured interview. For example, if the purpose of the interview is to collect information to be used in strategic planning, then the consultant/manager may want information from the upper level management team concerning such areas as follows:

- Clarity of the organization's mission

- How members see their contribution to the mission
- How members see the effectiveness of how the organization makes decisions, handles problems, rewards individual achievement, and so forth.
- Perceptions of strengths and weaknesses of the organization

The data from the interview and other collected information (e.g., questionnaires) provide the material to be worked upon in the planning sessions and are fed back to the group through handouts, summary charts, and verbatim reports. It is important to protect the privacy of the individuals being interviewed. Summarizing the data usually provides this protection. The interviewees need to know the purpose of the interview and how the information they provide will be handled. Decisions can be made during the interview as to what information the interviewee is willing to own in the planning sessions and what information they want to be kept private. The consultant should respect these wishes.

The structured interview presented here represents some of the information collected for a data feedback survey by the authors. Managers can modify or change items to suit their own organizational needs.

INTERVIEW QUESTIONNAIRE

Questions to be used during interviews at ___

Organization—Mission/Task/Processes

1. What is ___ mission, and how does your task (job) relate to the mission? What is your task?

2. How successful do you feel ___ has been in achieving its mission?
   Very unsuccessful   Very successful

   | 1 | 2 | 3 | 4 | 5 | 6 |

Explain:

3. How could ___ be *more* successful in achieving its mission?

4. What are the factors at ___ that unnecessarily limit your performance and/or the performance of others?

5. What are the factors at ___ that facilitate your performance and/or the performance of others?

6. Suggest a new idea or procedure that would (if adopted) spur yourself or others to increase performance.

7. What do you think of the problem-solving process at ___?

      Very ineffective   Very effective

         1   2   3   4   5   6

Explain:

8. In what way could the problem-solving process at ___ be improved?

9. What do you think of the decision-making process at ___?

      Very ineffective   Very effective

         1   2   3   4   5   6

Explain:

10. In what way could the decision-making process at ___ be improved?

11. How are differences or disagreements handled when they arise?

12. Is there feedback to persons who "get out of line" or "have problems"?
Give an example:

13. What is it about ___ that keeps people here?

14. What is it about ___ that is not attractive to the people here, or might cause them to leave?

Individual and Group Relationships (where line/staff divisions are not appropriate, substitute "departments," "disciplines," or other entities that are more appropriate to your organization.) Check one: Staff ___ Line ___

15. Describe the relationships *between* line and staff groups.

      Poor   Excellent

         1   2   3   4   5   6

Explain:

(a) Is there a spirit of helping and supporting?

      Little or none   Very much

         1   2   3   4   5   6

Describe:

(b) Is there much sharing of resources?

      Little or none   Very much

         1   2   3   4   5   6

Describe:

16. Describe the relationships *within* your (staff/line) group.

Poor					Excellent
1	2	3	4	5	6

Explain:

(a) Describe the degree of helping within your (staff/line) group.

None or very little					Very much
1	2	3	4	5	6

Describe:

(b) Describe the degree of *sharing* within your (staff/line) group.

None or very little					Very much
1	2	3	4	5	6

Describe:

17. What is the level of caring in this organization as a whole?

None or very little					Very much
1	2	3	4	5	6

Explain:

18. Using descriptive words or phrases, how would you describe the *line* manager's group as a group (your image of them)? Complete 18, 19, 20, and 21 if staff.

19. How would you describe your own group (what is your description of your own group's image)?

20. How free do you feel to ask for help from persons in the *line* organization?

Not at all					Very much
1	2	3	4	5	6

Explain:

21. How frequently do you *actually ask* for help from the *line* organization?

Seldom					Often
1	2	3	4	5	6

Explain:

22. Using descriptive words or phrases, how would you describe the *staff* group as a group (your image of them)?

Complete 22, 23, 24, and 25 if line.

23. How would you describe your own group as a group (self-image)?

24. How free do you feel to ask for help from persons in the *staff* group?

Not at all					Very much
1	2	3	4	5	6

Explain:

25. How frequently do you *actually ask* for help from the *staff* organization?

Seldom					Often
1	2	3	4	5	6

Utilization of Individuals
Please circle the appropriate number on each item.

26. How "in" do you feel on important company matters?

Not "in" at all					Very "in"
1	2	3	4	5	6

27. How "in" would you like to feel on important company matters?

Not at all					Very much
1	2	3	4	5	6

How much influence do you feel you have on the following items?
(Circle appropriate number)

28. Policy decisions affecting your areas of work?

No influence					Very influential
1	2	3	4	5	6

29. Operating decisions affecting your area of work?

No influence					Very influential
1	2	3	4	5	6

30. With superiors?

No influence					Very influential
1	2	3	4	5	6

31. With subordinates?

No influence					Very influential
1	2	3	4	5	6

32. With peers?

    No influence   Very influential

     1   2   3   4   5   6

33. With staff personnel?

    No influence   Very influential

     1   2   3   4   5   6

34. With line personnel?

    No influence   Very influential

     1   2   3   4   5   6

35. In personnel decisions?

    No influence   Very influential

     1   2   3   4   5   6

36. Decision Making: You are requested to list the three most important decisions made in your area of responsibility in the past year. After writing each decision in the space provided, please rank order the decision; assign #1 to the most important decision and #3 to the least significant decision.

36a. Decision:

    Rank

    #

How involved were you in making this decision? (circle appropriate number) How involved *should* you have been in making this decision? (Place a square around appropriate number.)

    No involvement   Very involved

     1   2   3   4   5   6

36b. Decision:

    Rank

    #

How involved were you in making this decision? (circle appropriate number) How involved *should* you have been in making this decision? (Place a square around appropriate number.)

    No involvement   Very involved

     1   2   3   4   5   6

36c. Decision:

    Rank

    #

How involved were you in making this decision? (circle appropriate number) How involved *should* you have been in making this decision? (Place a square around appropriate number.)

	No involvement				Very involved
1	2	3	4	5	6

Census of Decision-Making Procedures

When groups or work teams meet to accomplish some purpose, many kinds of decisions are made throughout the meeting. Some of these decisions are clear to all group members; many, however, are subtle and are easily ignored or are not obvious to all group members. However subtle, and regardless of how many members are involved or how the decisions are made, they affect group behavior in terms of subsequent commitment, productivity, and morale. A decision may range from merely changing the topic under discussion to deciding how the group will function, to decisions directly affecting future productivity. The purpose of this census is to sensitize team members to the types of decisions that take place during any team meetings and the possible consequences of these decisions on the level of participation, team members' feelings, and the direction in which the team is moving. The actual decision-making items are taken from a "plop to consensus" word list by Blake and Mouton (1962). The format and descriptions were developed by the present authors.

CENSUS OF DECISION-MAKING PROCEDURES

Below are descriptions of several styles of decisions that occur in team meetings. On the basis of *the session your team just completed*, please circle the number on each scale that best expresses your impression of how often that particular style of decision occurred. The number that you circle for each decision style will represent your subjective impression of approximately *how often* it occurred, and not necessarily the *actual number* of times that particular style of decision was utilized. Document your rating with specific examples of that decision style and who in the team was involved in them.

1. Plop: Individuals make contributions or suggestions but receive no response. Their ideas are rejected through silence and/or are ignored or passed over by the team so that they have no effect on team direction.

None at all	Once or twice	Several times	Many times	A great many times
1	2	3	4	5

Examples:

2. Self-Authorized: Individuals make suggestions or unilateral decisions without checking for reactions or needs of other team members. No one objects or offers an alternative, and the team behaves, temporarily, as if they support the decision.

				A great
None at all	Once or twice	Several times	Many times	many times
1	2	3	4	5

Example:

3. Handclasp: One or more individuals support the suggestion or decision of another team member. Needs of other group members are not checked. The two people involved in the handclasp may think they have the team's support when they may not.

				A great
None at all	Once or twice	Several times	Many times	many times
1	2	3	4	5

Example:

5. Majority Support: More than half the team is in agreement about a decision and overrides or outvotes the minority. The minority may go along on the surface but block team action later because they had no part in the decision.

				A great
None at all	Once or twice	Several times	Many times	many times
1	2	3	4	5

Example:

6. Compromise: Team members cannot fully agree on a decision, so each member or side sacrifices something in order to get the job done. A climate of uneasiness results because no one got what they really wanted.

				A great
None at all	Once or twice	Several times	Many times	many times
1	2	3	4	5

Example:

7. Near-Consensus: All but one or two members are in agreement and will support the decision. They have had a chance to express themselves and feel understood.

Satisfaction is high, but dissenting members may not be completely happy with the decision.

None at all	Once or twice	Several times	Many times	A great many times
1	2	3	4	5

Example:

8. Polling: Checking with all members of the team to see where they stand on an action or decision. This procedure does *not commit* team members to a decision. They may be testing for consensus, but no decision is actually made.

None at all	Once or twice	Several times	Many times	A great many times
1	2	3	4	5

Example:

9. Consensus: All members are in agreement, both in thought and feeling, about a decision. All members are heard from. This kind of decision takes longer, but when it is accomplished, satisfaction and commitment are very high.

None at all	Once or twice	Several times	Many times	A great many times
1	2	3	4	5

Example:

Postmeeting Questionnaires

Postmeeting questionnaires are useful tools to facilitate the processing of *how* the group or team worked during the session just completed. They provide a point of departure from the content of the team meeting and enable members to express their feelings and thoughts about their own participation and the participation of others. Once these feelings and thoughts are surfaced and discussed, corrective goals can be set for subsequent meetings.

Many managers or team leaders do not like to set aside time for processing the meeting because "it takes time." What frequently happens then is that team members will express their thoughts and feelings about the meeting outside the session, where they cannot be resolved as a team issue. Once a team is practiced in discussing its own process, meetings tend to be more open and more satisfying, and there is a greater tendency to catch process issues as they occur in the session. This type of ongoing activity increases the productivity of the team. All the information, thoughts, and feelings critical to effective decision making and problem solving are on the table.

The last two questionnaires involve personal goal setting for the member about behaviors he or she wants to try out during the meeting. The questionnaires also indicate a way to get feedback from other members about the extent to which the personal goals were met.

Name_____

Date_____

PERSONAL REACTION FORM

Instructions: Please respond to the following statements on the basis of your feelings and reactions to the decision your group has developed. Answer as objectively and honestly as possible.

A. To what extent did you participate in the group decision?
 1. Not at all
 2. Slightly
 3. Some
 4. About average
 5. Moderately
 6. Quite a lot
 7. Totally
B. How satisfied are you with your level of participation?
 1. Completely dissatisfied
 2. Mostly dissatisfied
 3. Somewhat dissatisfied
 4. Neutral
 5. Somewhat satisfied
 6. Mostly satisfied
 7. Completely satisfied
C. To what extent do you feel responsible for the decisions reached by your group?
 1. Totally not responsible
 2. Mostly not responsible
 3. Moderately not responsible
 4. Neutral
 5. Moderately responsible

6. Quite responsible
7. Totally responsible

D. How committed do you feel to the decisions made by your group?
1. Uncommitted
2. Quite uncommitted
3. Mostly uncommitted
4. Neutral
5. Mostly committed
6. Quite committed
7. Totally committed

E. How frustrating was this task for you personally?
1. Completely frustrating experience
2. Quite frustrating
3. Moderately frustrating
4. Neutral
5. Moderately positive
6. Quite positive
7. Totally positive

F. How good were your group decisions?
1. The worst possible decision
2. A really bad decision
3. A poor decision
4. A fair decision
5. A good decision
6. An outstanding decision
7. The best possible decision

Name_____
Date_____

POSTMEETING QUESTIONNAIRE

Instructions: Circle the number under each item that best describes your feelings and reactions to the team meeting.

1. How much influence did you feel you had on the decision making?

Very little   Very much

1	2	3	4	5	6	7

2. How often did you feel your team members really listened to you in the meeting?

Very little   Very much

1	2	3	4	5	6	7

3. How much cooperation and collaboration did you feel took place?

Very little   Very much

1	2	3	4	5	6	7

4. To what extent were members open and honest with each other about their thoughts, feelings, and attitudes?

None   Great deal

1	2	3	4	5	6	7

5. How committed are you to the decisions that the team made?

Strongly committed   Strongly uncommitted

1	2	3	4	5	6	7

6. How do you feel about the way your team worked on the assignment?

Highly dissatisfied   Highly satisfied

1	2	3	4	5	6	7

7. Select one word describing the climate of your group.

Name_____

Date_____

POSTMEETING QUESTIONNAIRE

Instructions: Circle the number on each item that best describes your perception of this team's session.

1. Inclusion:

Completely excluded   Completely included

| 1 | 2 | 3 | 4 | 5 | 6 | 7 |

2. Commitment:

How much commitment do you now feel to your group?

Completely uncommitted   Completely committed

| 1 | 2 | 3 | 4 | 5 | 6 | 7 |

3. Product:

How do you feel about the quality of your group's product or discussion?

Completely dissatisfied   Completely satisfied

| 1 | 2 | 3 | 4 | 5 | 6 | 7 |

4. Resources:

To what extent did your group utilize its resources?

Not utilized at all   Complete utilization

| 1 | 2 | 3 | 4 | 5 | 6 | 7 |

PERSONAL GOALS SCALE

For the upcoming team meeting, *indicate your intentions* about your own participation by circling the appropriate number under each item. After the meeting you may want to check with other members to see to what extent you reached your goal.

1. Openness (feelings, perceptions):

Not expressing or sharing   Expressing feelings as
here-and-now feelings.   they are occurring.

| 1 | 2 | 3 | 4 | 5 | 6 | 7 |

2. Risk taking (confronting others, stating where you are, experimenting):

                                                 Completely willing to
Play it safe all the time.   stick my neck out.

| 1 | 2 | 3 | 4 | 5 | 6 | 7 |

3. Supporting others (making supportive statements):

Not checking to see where others are or how they are feeling.				Checking to see where others are or how they are feeling.		
1	2	3	4	5	6	7

4. Gatekeeping (soliciting participation by members who have low participation or have been cut off):

Not checking how and if others are participating.				Checking to see who is not participating. Encouraging others to talk.		
1	2	3	4	5	6	7

PERSONAL GOALS FOR THIS MEETING

Under each goal, circle the number that best describes *your intention before the group meeting.* After meeting, circle the number that best describes the *extent to which you met your goals.* You may share these ratings with others and get their feedback. Ask how they saw your behavior in relation to the items during the meeting.

1. Do I actively listen to others? Hear people out? Try to understand? Ask for clarification?

Before: Not at all	1	2	3	4	5	Very much
After: Not at all	1	2	3	4	5	Very much

2. Do I try to draw others out? Help silent people to come in?

Before: Not at all	1	2	3	4	5	Very much
After: Not at all	1	2	3	4	5	Very much

3. Do I ask about and try to understand others' feelings?

Before: Not at all	1	2	3	4	5	Very much
After: Not at all	1	2	3	4	5	Very much

4. Do I tend to take charge of the group? Dominate? Crowd others out?

Before: Very much	1	2	3	4	5	Not at all
After: Very much	1	2	3	4	5	Not at all

5. Do I tend to talk too much? Cut others off? Interrupt?

Before: Very much	1	2	3	4	5	Not at all
After: Very much	1	2	3	4	5	Not at all

6. Do I try to stay with the group? Avoid topic jumping or going off on tangents?

Before: Not at all	1	2	3	4	5	Very much
After: Not at all	1	2	3	4	5	Very much

7. Do I tend to be silent? Not speaking my mind? Not letting others know where I stand?

Before: Very much	1	2	3	4	5	Not at all
After: Very much	1	2	3	4	5	Not at all

8. Do I tend to speak for myself and not for others, encouraging others to do the same?

Before: Very much	1	2	3	4	5	Not at all
After: Very much	1	2	3	4	5	Not at all

9. Do I try to express my own feelings?

Before: Not at all	1	2	3	4	5	Very much
After: Not at all	1	2	3	4	5	Very much

A Sample OD Project:
Survey Data Feedback

The following description of a Survey Data Feedback (SDF) project reflects the definition of an OD technology more than a full OD program. The effort involved (a) a felt need on the part of the client to do a diagnostic assessment of the state of the organization and (b) participation of the client in developing the project. The third criterion (Burke, 1994), a change in the culture of the organization, was not evident. If the data collected had shown evidence of significant issues or disparities and the management team had decided to engage in a corrective effort, then the SDF would have represented a first step in an OD program. A cultural change might then have been evident as a consequence of the OD interventions. For the purposes of this exposition, we will not go into the details of the measurements and interactions, but present an outline of the goals and design.

The company was a gas exploration arm of a larger oil-related organization. It consisted of several hundred employees and was managed by a president (CEO), five staff managers, and seven line managers. These 13 individuals constituted the top management team. The first meeting of the consultant and the president was arranged by an internal training officer. The consultant had worked with the training officer on several previous occasions. The president was curious as to how "things were going" in his company. The consultant suggested a survey data feedback session and roughly outlined the steps and how the information collected would be handled. The consultant asked the president to be more specific about his "curiosity." Both president and consultant developed an outline of objectives or purposes for the SDF. We might add, at this point, that the president had already discussed the use of a consultant with his management team. Some of his contributions to the purposes of the project included their suggestions.

Purposes of the SDF—to provide an opportunity

1. For management to see, in a more objective and organized way, how they currently view the organization.
2. To compare the perceptions of each manager and the president with the perceptions of other team members.
3. To compare the images (stereotypes) each group (line vs. staff) had of the other, and the effect of these stereotypes on intergroup relations.
4. To identify some trends or locate some issues, disparities, strengths, weaknesses, and so on, that might be analyzed and discussed by the team.
5. For managers to work through the data they produced and to tease out some meaning and understanding of the information and the process. A desirable by-product would be an educational experience for the managers.
6. For managers to decide what they want to do with the information. The survey itself required no commitment to action. It could be used for informational purposes only. The nature of the data feedback to the managers would probably determine what, if any, action would be taken.

Data collection and collation

1. Interview data
    a. Conducted structured interviews (see sample in Appendix A) with the president and the 12 managers. This process took about 3 days.
    b. Collated and transcribed all individual responses, item by item. Tallied and computed averages and ranges for all scalar items.
    c. Summarized all responses for each item in terms of frequency of appearance by line, staff, and total groups.
    d. Grouped interview data into related clusters for team and subgroups to work on and present to total team. Included rating scales and summary presentations of findings.
2. Mailed questionnaires
    a. Sent to the 12 managers who were interviewed. Some scaled items were suggested by information arising from the interviews. This procedure cut down interview time and produced scaled or rating-type information.
    b. Tallied responses and computed averages and ranges for each item by line, staff, and total groups.

   c. Constructed tables and charts from the statistical analysis and clustered
      interview items.
3. Data grouping: sources of groupings (i.e., interview and mailed questionnaire
   item numbers) are not all included in this outline. Most interview items appear
   in Appendix A: *Structured Interview—Interview Questionnaire* (pp. 148-154, this
   volume). Mailed questionnaire item headings are included, but not the scales
   themselves.

   a. Mission statement and performance of organization:

      Interview items: 1-6

      Mailed questionnaire items: 16 (objectives), 20 (innovation), 21 (flexibility
      of structure), 24 (individual growth), 25 (feedback on performance)

   b. Problem solving, decision making, and mistakes:

      Interview items: 7-10; 11 and 12

      Mailed questionnaire items: 18 (problem solving), 22 (decision making),
      26 (handling conflict), 28 (decision involvement)

   c. Interpersonal/intergroup climate and sharing of resources:

      Interview items: 13-17; 20-25

      Mailed questionnaire items: 17 (openness), 19 (commitment), 23 (mutual
      support)

   d. Images (stereotypes) of staff and line groups:

      Interview items: 18, 19, 22, and 23

   e. Utilization of resources:

      Interview items: 26-36

      Mailed questionnaire items: 27 (resource utilization)

Data feedback

1. Constructed packet of all findings to be distributed to each member of the
   management team.
2. Set up series of flip charts around the conference room. Consultant presented
   the data from the structured interviews and the mailed questionnaires. Walked
   around the room from chart to chart.
3. Managers discussed the findings from each presentation and made notes in their
   packets in preparation for presenting the information to their own subordinate
   teams.

Subgroup work teams

1. Formed subgroup work teams to analyze the data with which they chose to
   work. They were to select the most significant information, list on newsprint,
   and present to the total team.

2. Team presentation and discussion.
3. Managers decided priorities as to how they wanted to use the data and what information they should bring back to the follow-up management team meeting from their subordinate teams.
4. Set target dates to present to subordinate teams and follow-up management team meeting. Follow-up team meeting would include information and feedback from subordinate team meetings, and would make decisions concerning next step.

Wrap-up and evaluation

The SDF session took a full day. In the follow-up session the president and the managers decided not to go any further at the present time. The data from the SDF session and from the subordinate team sessions showed no significant problem areas. They felt that the minor discrepancies that had surfaced were manageable now that they were more aware of them. In retrospect, we should have asked the question, "Do you think you can do better?" rather than settling for a comfortable status quo. They may have reoriented themselves and the data to a future perspective. The primary benefits from the survey were two: From their perspectives, the clients obtained an overview of the organization; and they felt they had received an education on how to conduct future diagnoses of their organization.

APPENDIX C

Self-Assessment Monitoring Program for Managers, Trainers, and OD Consultants

Throughout this book we have referred to many skills, technologies, and behavioral theories that consultants and aspiring consultants possess or are in the process of developing. Development, for many of them, means accruing more techniques, concepts, and knowledge about the field of OD and training to keep them current in the profession. There is much less focus on personal development and increased self-awareness. This is unfortunate when we consider that the most important asset consultants, or any helpers (trainers, therapists), bring to a client are themselves—who they are as people, and their values, personal biases, expectations, attitudes, and motivations.

OD shares with other helping professions a crucial interaction between personal and technical skills and understanding. Consultants who are highly skilled and knowledgeable in the technical areas but lack self-awareness and interpersonal sensitivity may do more harm than good in their attempts to facilitate change in others. Little or no self-awareness may result in an insensitivity to their impact on others, a lack of discrimination between their own needs and the needs of the client, and a lack of appreciation of their own style of leadership and its effect on the client system. On the positive side, frequent experiences in learning events that increase self-awareness and deepen personal insights can rejuvenate busy consultants and prevent consultant burnout. There are many opportunities to engage in personal

AUTHORS' NOTE: This appendix was modified from an article by Hanson and Lubin (1987).

development activities (T-group participation, co-training with an experienced trainer, encouraging feedback from group or team members, taking experiential workshops on leadership and OD consultation, creating one's own "development group" at work or in the community).

The purpose of this appendix is to present a program in which self-development can be monitored by the managers or consultants themselves. The underlying assumption of the program is that you are interested in and highly motivated to gain a deeper awareness of your own personal and professional style and to integrate these facets of yourself into your work with clients.

To facilitate this self-development program, several sets of scales are presented to assist you to identify and think about important consultant behaviors, skills, knowledge, and attitudes. The items represent a sample of behaviors reflecting areas of personal, interpersonal, communication, group, and leadership skills. The scales can be modified or items can be added to or deleted to suit your needs and the situations in which you find yourself. Each item should be considered thoughtfully in order to assess "where you are now" and "where you would like to be." Items of most interest can be checked with other individuals who know you well enough to give valid feedback.

The sample of scales is primarily a self-assessment vehicle to alert you to various dimensions of your own behaviors and an awareness of the extent to which you practice them. The last scale is an assessment of how *others* perceive your leadership behaviors in a group or team setting. The present scales were abstracted from Hanson and Lubin (1980). The areas presented represent 4 (not including the leadership scales) of 10 areas of the instrument. The other areas are Giving and Receiving Feedback, Group Observation Skills, Support Systems, Handling Negative Feelings, Risk Taking, and General: A Way of Being. The scales included here cover areas such as

- Awareness of self—the extent to which you are aware of your own feelings; body sensations; patterns of thought; attitudes and expectations; reactions to criticism, praise, and frustration; and discrimination between observations and interpretations—your internal focus of attention.

- Awareness of others—the extent to which you are aware of the expression of others' feelings (verbal and nonverbal, direct vs. indirect); handle emotional situations; differentiate between feelings and thoughts; and notice body language, style of verbal expression, reactions to feedback, thought patterns (reference points in time), and repetitive themes—your external focus of attention.

- Interpersonal relations—the extent to which you are aware of *how* you manage your interpersonal transactions—initiating contacts; trusting self and others; handling disagreements; being dominating, deferential, open, confronting, competitive, or cooperative; expressing feelings and thoughts (both positive and negative); and wanting attention.

- Communication—the extent to which you are aware of *how* you communicate—telling others your own feelings and thoughts, clarity of intentions, listening and hearing others out, responding to what is communicated, checking for understanding, focusing on what others say rather than on your own thoughts, handling unclear communications, and reading motivation behind what is communicated.

- Team/group leader feedback—the extent to which team or group members perceive you along a variety of leadership behavioral dimensions—accepting feelings and thoughts being expressed; accepting feedback from team members; giving feedback to members; creating a supportive climate; sharing leadership; listening and checking out perceptions; and being willing to express your own feelings and thoughts, aware of group process, accessible, and nonjudgmental.

Throughout the scales we have used the word *noting*. Where it is not used, it is implied. Noting is an Eastern concept of staying alert to whatever is happening in the here and now without judging, interpreting, or evaluating the experience. It is being with the experience of the present moment and attending to (not analyzing) whatever arises in that moment. The process of noting reduces the contamination from judging, interpreting, or analyzing, and helps to keep the figure sharp and clear, distinct from its surrounding ground. It allows emerging and submerging perceptions and feelings to flow without hindering them.

SELF-ASSESSMENT SCALES AND GOALS FOR PERSONAL DEVELOPMENT

Very few people will disagree that increasing personal effectiveness is an ideal goal. In setting such goals, however, we tend to be very vague, making them too global to implement or too idealistic to attain (e.g., communicate better, be an effective person). This program attempts to be more practical and realistic by specifying areas of personal development and identifying specific behaviors within those areas. Once a sampling of behaviors within each area has been identified, you can then assess your own status or level as it is now. In setting goals, we need to ascertain where we are now on a particular dimension before we can pinpoint where we would like to be. The behaviors we are addressing are not easily defined or agreed upon, and are often perceived as highly subjective. Using scales for these behaviors objectifies the assessment and enables you to measure movement toward or away from your goals. In addition, guessing how other people see you provides an anchor for the self-assessment, making it more realistic. You can then check out your "guess" with the people who know you.

The program serves another purpose. The scales may stimulate you to examine your own interpersonal style and to explore aspects of yourself that have been previously overlooked.

The following pages contain a sampling of goal items that will, it is hoped, help you to think about different aspects of yourself in relation to others, to groups or teams in which you hold membership, and to the organization in which you work.

   a. Read through the lists and *circle* the number on each scale that best represents the extent to which you do the activity described (i.e., how you see yourself *now*).

   b. Draw a *square* around the number on each scale that represents where you would *like to be*.

   c. Place a *check mark* over the number on each scale that represents a guess as to how other people see you on that item.

   d. Do not hesitate to add items that are not listed but that you feel are important.

   e. Go over the list and check three or four goals that you would like to work on at this time. A goal may include a cluster of items that are related to each other.

Goals:

Extent to which:
- O   I do this now
- □   I would like to do this more, or less
- ✓   Others see me doing this

I. Awareness of Self

	Not at all				Very much
1. Noting how I am feeling	1	2	3	4	5
2. Noting my body sensations	1	2	3	4	5
3. Noting my body postures, gestures, and movements	1	2	3	4	5
4. Noting any spontaneous or involuntary imagery that occurs in my "mind's eye"	1	2	3	4	5
5. Noting stream and patterns of thoughts as they occur	1	2	3	4	5
6. Noting what attitudes or expectations are present toward myself	1	2	3	4	5
7. Noting what attitudes or expectations are present toward others	1	2	3	4	5
8. Noting what criticisms, evaluations, or judgments I make about myself	1	2	3	4	5

	Not at all			Very much	
9. Noting what criticisms, evaluations, or judgments I make about others	1	2	3	4	5
10. Noting whether I give reasons, explanations, or justifications for my behavior	1	2	3	4	5
11. Noting to what extent I am owning and accepting my feelings, attitudes, beliefs, and so on	1	2	3	4	5
12. Noting how I react to praise or criticism	1	2	3	4	5
13. Noting how I react to being assisted or helped	1	2	3	4	5
14. Noting how I react to being hindered or blocked	1	2	3	4	5
15. Noting differences when I am making an observation (e.g., you are frowning) or an interpretation (e.g., you are angry) of another's behavior	1	2	3	4	5

II. Awareness of Others

	Not at all			Very much	
1. Noting the feelings of others	1	2	3	4	5
2. Noting through what media feelings are expressed (e.g., verbal, nonverbal)	1	2	3	4	5
3. Noting differences between expression of feelings versus thoughts or perceptions	1	2	3	4	5
4. Noting how others handle feelings that are expressed to them	1	2	3	4	5
5. Noting body postures, movements, facial expressions	1	2	3	4	5
6. Noting style of verbal expression (e.g., tone, rapid/slow, soft/loud, rising/ dropping, gesturing, incomplete sentences)	1	2	3	4	5
7. Noting shifts in style of verbal expression	1	2	3	4	5
8. Noting to what extent others use observations versus interpretations as a way of describing behavior	1	2	3	4	5
9. Noting to what extent others judge or evaluate, instead of describing, behavior	1	2	3	4	5

	Not at all				Very much
10. Noting how others receive feedback (e.g., defending or explaining their behavior vs. asking for clarification, checking with others, accepting openly)	1	2	3	4	5
11. Noting most frequent reference points (e.g., self, others, past, present, future) in others' communication	1	2	3	4	5
12. Noting how others handle emotional situations such as praise, conflict, closeness, anger, affection, and so on	1	2	3	4	5
13. Noting to what extent others express feelings directly (e.g., "I like you")	1	2	3	4	5
14. Noting to what extent others express feelings indirectly (e.g., "You are likable")	1	2	3	4	5
15. Noting repetitive themes that are characteristic of others (e.g., always making comparisons, undervaluing self or others)	1	2	3	4	5

III. **Interpersonal Relations**

	Not at all				Very much
1. I initiate contacts with other people rather than wait for them to come to me	1	2	3	4	5
2. My style is to trust others or give the benefit of the doubt	1	2	3	4	5
3. I find it difficult to say "no" to others	1	2	3	4	5
4. I don't like people to get too close to me	1	2	3	4	5
5. In any disagreement I push to get my way	1	2	3	4	5
6. In my relationships with others I tend to dominate	1	2	3	4	5
7. I tend to be deferential in my relationships with others	1	2	3	4	5
8. In most of my relationships I am open, expressing my feelings freely	1	2	3	4	5
9. I encourage others to express their feelings, both positive and negative, toward me	1	2	3	4	5
10. I stand my ground firmly when I feel I am misunderstood or not being heard	1	2	3	4	5

	Not at all			Very much

11. In many of my relationships I feel competitive with others, and it is important for me to be right   1   2   3   4   5

12. People come to me for advice and counsel   1   2   3   4   5

13. If I feel I am being used or taken advantage of, I will speak up and confront the other person   1   2   3   4   5

14. I express my feelings (both positive and negative) toward others   1   2   3   4   5

15. In the company of others I like attention   1   2   3   4   5

IV. Communication

1. Telling others what I think   1   2   3   4   5

2. Telling others how I feel   1   2   3   4   5

3. Being clear on what I intend to communicate   1   2   3   4   5

4. Striving to understand others   1   2   3   4   5

5. Listening attentively to what others are saying   1   2   3   4   5

6. Hearing others out   1   2   3   4   5

7. Drawing others out   1   2   3   4   5

8. Giving an indication that I heard what was said   1   2   3   4   5

9. Asking for clarification when I'm not sure I understand   1   2   3   4   5

10. Repeating back to make certain I heard the communication correctly   1   2   3   4   5

11. Stopping the noise in my own head (i.e., thinking about what I'm going to say, judging, evaluating) and focusing on the other person   1   2   3   4   5

12. Noting my attitudes and intentions when I am not communicating clearly   1   2   3   4   5

13. Noting how and when I slant my communication in order for it to be what I think the other person wants to hear   1   2   3   4   5

14. Noting how and when I slant my communication in order for others to accept the image I want to project   1   2   3   4   5

	Not at all				Very much

15. Noting the process (how we are communicating) of communication as well as the content (what we are communicating)   1   2   3   4   5

V. Team/Group Leader Feedback

Rate your group leader on each item below according to the following scale:

1. Very little of the time
2. Some of the time
3. A little less than half of the time
4. About half and half
5. A little more than half of the time
6. Most of the time
7. Almost all of the time

____ Leader attends to, and accepts, feelings that group members express

____ Leader appears open and receptive; is able to accept feedback about his or her own behavior

____ Leader listens carefully to what group members say; asks for clarification or checks for understanding.

____ Leader expresses his or her own feelings, even when negative

____ Leader helps others to express their feelings, both positive and negative

____ Leader keeps group on target; brings group members back to topic or issue when they wander

____ Leader responds openly and frankly; you know where he or she stands

____ Leader handles conflict and strong feelings directly; does not change subject or smooth over the problem

____ Leader is aware of and understands what is going on in the group

____ Leader is willing to take risks; confronts others, takes a stand, sticks neck out

____ Leader is supportive of group members; checks to see where others are or how they are feeling

____ Leader checks to see who is not participating; encourages silent members to talk

____ Leader is warm and easy to approach; does not appear distant and aloof

____ Leader is willing to share leadership with group members; accepts ideas and suggestions and acts on them

___ Leader expresses him- or herself clearly, is easily understood

___ Leader appears comfortable in the group; has an air of self-confidence and appears to trust his of her own judgment

___ Leader is objective and nonjudgmental; does not evaluate others as right or wrong, good or bad

___ Leader explores own feelings, values, and perceptions of self when relevant to the group; processing always includes his or her own here-and-now experiences when appropriate to the group

Comments: _____

_____

_____

Review the ratings you have made of yourself and the ratings you received from others. Some of these items may fall into naturally related clusters. Asterisk those items that you would like to earmark as goals to be worked on. List the goals on the *Goals Monitoring Worksheet* and rank them in the order of which ones you want to work on first. Then ask yourself the following questions (jot down your responses):

    a. Is there a common thread running through the goals? Can I group them according to some underlying commonalities?

    b. Are there any that tend to be general as opposed to specific situations? That is, are they typical of me in a variety of situations, or do some crop up only in specific situations? If the latter is true, describe these situations.

    c. If I work on one goal, how will it affect the others?

    d. What are some events (e.g., a T-group, a staff meeting, support or resource person, a workshop, group therapy) coming up at which I can test some of these goals?

    e. Who can I use as a resource or support person to get feedback on these goals?

Assessing Goals and Planning Program:

    a. Once you have listed the goals and ranked them, place an "x" on the scale opposite the goal (i.e., Hi., Med., Low.) reflecting where you see yourself *now*. Do this rating for each goal in the column under *now*. You can judge, from the self-assessment scales presented above, where (low, medium, high) you rated yourself on an item.

    b. Identify the next event you will be attending at which you can test or get feedback on some of these goals. Decide which goals will be relevant to the event. Note this event as Checkpoint 1 on the *Checkpoint Identification Chart,* specifying where and when the event will occur. Specify goal(s) by placing the designated letter(s) (e.g., A, B, C) from the Goals Monitoring Worksheet in the appropriate column (i.e., goal) on the Checkpoint Identification Chart. Note that more than one goal can be implemented during a single checkpoint. Also date the event so that you will have a record of times between events ("When" column).

GOALS MONITORING WORKSHEET

Rank	Goal					Checkpoints			
		Now	1	2	3	4	5	6	7
___ A.	High / Medium / Low								
___ B.	High / Medium / Low								
___ C.	High / Medium / Low								
___ D.	High / Medium / Low								
___ E.	High / Medium / Low								
___ F.	High / Medium / Low								

CHECKPOINT IDENTIFICATION CHART

Checkpoint	Goal(s)	Situation	Where	When
1.				
2.				
3.				
4.				

Checkpoint	Goal(s)	Situation	Where	When

5._____

6._____

7._____

    c. Develop your plan as to how you will get the feedback on your goals at the first checkpoint. Use only scales relevant to the goals you are testing and have people rate you.

    d. After you have collected the data for Checkpoint 1, make a judgment concerning where on the scale (Goals Monitoring Worksheet) the data reflect your ratings and place an "x" on low, medium, or high.

    e. Repeat the process for Checkpoints 2, 3, and so on when they occur.

    f. Finally, you need to set criteria as to when you have achieved a goal (e.g., two or three "high" ratings on consecutive checkpoints). Remember, once you have achieved your criterion on a goal, this does not mean that you can forget that goal. Ignoring goals that have been achieved can result in slippage from "high" to "low." Growth is a never-ending process of setting goals, implementing them, getting feedback, achieving them, and continuously monitoring behaviors reflecting these goals.

The format may be modified to suit your particular needs. Busy managers, trainers, and OD consultants working this program may find it time consuming at first. After completing one round of assessments and goal setting, the process will take less time. Self-examination may be unsettling at times, but is rarely a waste of time. To "know thyself" is the first critical step to knowing others. The key ingredient is the motivation of the manager, trainer, or consultant and his or her commitment to a self-development program. Without this commitment, the most sophisticated development program is useless, not to mention the time, energy, and creativity required to implement it. It is incumbent upon professionals in the helping professions to subject themselves to the same self-scrutiny that they encourage for their clients. Accepting the charge of learning about yourself and, as a consequence, increasing your sensitivity to others, is one of the hallmark values of organization development.

References

Albrecht, K. (1983). *Organization development: A total systems approach to positive change in any business organization*. Englewood Cliffs, NJ: Prentice Hall.

American Productivity and Quality Center. (1992). *Total quality improvement awareness*. Houston: Author.

Argyris, C. (1957). *Personality and organizations*. New York: Harper-Collins.

Argyris, C. (1970). *Intervention theory and method*. Reading, MA: Addison-Wesley.

Argyris, C. (1990). *Overcoming organizational defenses: Facilitating organizational learning*. Needham, MA: Allyn & Bacon.

Argyris, C. (1993). *Knowledge for action*. San Francisco: Jossey-Bass.

Bales, R. F. (1958). Task roles and social roles in problem solving groups. In E. E. MacCoby, T. M. Newcomb, & G. L. Hartley (Eds.), *Readings in social psychology* (pp. 437-447). New York: Holt, Rinehart & Winston.

Bales, R. F. (1970). *Personality and interpersonal behavior*. New York: Simon & Schuster.

Bass, B. M. (1962). *The orientation inventory: Manual* (research ed.). Palo Alto, CA: Consulting Psychologists Press.

Bass, B. M. (1967). Social behavior and the orientation inventory: A review. *Psychological Bulletin, 64,* 260-292.

Beckhard, R., & Harris, R. (1977). *Organizational transitions: Managing complex change*. Reading, MA: Addison-Wesley.

Bell, R., Cleveland, S., Hanson, P. G., & O'Connell, W. E. (1969). Small group dialogue and discussion: An approach to police-community relationship. *Journal of Criminal Law, Criminology and Police Science, 60,* 242-245.

Benne, K. D. (1975). Conceptual and moral foundations of laboratory method. In K. D. Benne, L. P. Bradford, J. R. Gibb, & R. O. Lippitt (Eds.), *The laboratory method of changing and learning: Theory and application* (pp. 24-55). Palo Alto, CA: Science and Behavior Books.

Benne, K. D., Bradford, L. P., & Lippitt, R. (1964). The laboratory method. In L. P. Bradford, J. R. Gibb, & K. D. Benne (Eds.), *T-group theory and laboratory method: Innovation in re-education* (pp. 15-44). New York: John Wiley.

Benne, K. D., & Sheats, P. (1948). Functional roles of group members. *Journal of Social Issues, 4*(2), 41-49.

Bennis, W. G. (1966). *Changing organizations.* New York: McGraw-Hill.

Blake, R. R., & Mouton, J. S. (1962). The instrumented laboratory. In I. R. Weschler & E. H. Schein (Eds.), *Issues in human relations training: Selected reading series V* (pp. 61-76). Washington, DC: National Education Association, National Training Laboratories (currently the NTL Institute, Alexandria, VA).

Blake, R. R., & Mouton, J. S. (1964). *The managerial grid.* Houston: Gulf.

Blake, R. R., & Mouton, J. S. (1968). *Corporate excellence through grid organization development.* Houston, TX: Gulf.

Blake, R. R., & Mouton, J. S. (1976). *Consultation.* Reading, MA: Addison-Wesley.

Blake, R. R., & Mouton, J. S. (1983). *Consultation: A handbook for individual and organizational development* (2nd ed.). Reading, MA: Addison-Wesley.

Blake, R. R., Shepard, H. A., & Mouton, J. S. (1964). *Managing intergroup conflict in industry.* Houston, TX: Gulf.

Blank, R., & Slipp, S. (1994). *Voices of diversity.* New York: American Management Association.

Block, P. (1981). *Flawless consulting: A guide to getting your expertise used.* San Diego, CA: Pfeifer.

Bolen, J. S. (1979). *The Tao of psychology: Synchronicity and the self.* New York: Harper & Row.

Bradford, L. P., Gibb, J. R., & Benne, K. D. (Eds.). (1964). *T-group theory and laboratory method: Innovation in re-education.* New York: John Wiley.

Burke, W. W. (1994). *Organization development: A process of learning and changing* (2nd ed.). Reading, MA: Addison-Wesley.

Bynner, W. (1962). *The way of life according to Lao Tzu.* New York: Capricorn Books. [Translated by W. Bynner. Quoted by Carl R. Rogers. (1962). *A way of being.* (p. 42). Boston: Houghton Mifflin.]

Chisholm, R. F. (1983, March). Quality of working life: critical issue for the 80's. *Public Productivity Review,* pp. 10-25.

Clark, J. V. (1971). Motivation in work groups: A tentative view. In D. A. Kolb, I. M. Rubin, & J. M. McIntyre (Eds.), *Organizational psychology* (pp. 93-109). Englewood Cliffs, NJ: Prentice Hall.

Cobbs, P. M. (1944). The challenge and opportunities of diversity. In E. Y. Cross, J. H. Katz, F. A. Miller, & E. W. Seashore (Eds.), *The promise of diversity* (pp. 25-31). New York: Irwin.

Cotter, J., & Mohr, B. (1984). *Designing more effective organizations: An introduction to socio-technical systems.* North Hollywood, CA: John Cotter Associates & Bernard Mohr, Human Systems Consultants.

Crosby, P. B. (1979). *Quality is free: The art of making quality certain.* New York: McGraw-Hill.

Crosby, P. B. (1984). *Quality without tears.* New York: McGraw-Hill.

Cross, E. Y., Katz, J. H., Miller, F. A., & Seashore, E. W. (1994). *The promise of diversity.* New York: Irwin.

Deming, W. E. (1986). *Out of crisis.* Cambridge: MIT Center for Advanced Engineering Study.

Dyer, W. G. (1987). *Team building: Issues and alternatives* (2nd ed.). Reading, MA: Addison-Wesley.

Edelman, J., & Crain, M. B. (1993). *The Tao of negotiation.* New York: Harper Business.

Fordyce, J. K., & Weil, R. (1971). *Managing with people: A manager's handbook on organization development methods.* Reading, MA: Addison-Wesley.

French, W. L., & Bell, C. H., Jr. (1990). *Organization development: Behavioral science interventions for organization improvement* (4th ed.). Englewood Cliffs, NJ: Prentice Hall.

Gallessich, J. (1982). *The profession and practice of consultation: A handbook for consultants, trainers of consultants, and consumers of consultation services.* San Francisco: Jossey-Bass.

Grossman, L. (1974). *The change agent*. New York: American Management Association.

Hall, J. (Ed.). (1988). *Models for management: The structure of competence* (2nd ed.). The Woodlands, TX: Woodstead.

Hanson, P. G. (1973). *Individual and group effectiveness training: A handbook for trainers*. Washington, DC: Veterans Administration, Department of Medicine and Surgery.

Hanson, P. G. (1981). *Learning through groups: A trainer's basic guide*. San Diego, CA: University Associates.

Hanson, P. G., Baker, R. R., Paris, J., Brown-Burke, R. L., Ermalinski, R., & Dinardo, Q. E. (1977). *Training for individual and group effectiveness and resourcefulness: A handbook for trainers*. Washington, DC: Veterans Administration, Department of Medicine and Surgery.

Hanson, P. G., & Burke, A. R. (1977). *Diagnosing organizational effectiveness: A. How I see my organization; B. How I see my work unit or team*. Houston, TX: Authors.

Hanson, P. G., & Lubin, B. (1980). *Self assessment and goals for personal development*. Houston, TX: Hanlu Associates.

Hanson, P. G., & Lubin, B. (1986). Support systems: Understanding and using them effectively. *Organizational Development Journal, 4*(4), 59-66.

Hanson, P. G., & Lubin, B. (1987). Assessment of trainer skills by self, peers, and supervisors. In W. B. Reddy & C. C. Henderson (Eds.), *Training theory and practice* (pp. 47-56). San Diego, CA: University Associates.

Hanson, P. G., & Lubin, B. (1988). Team building as group development. In W. B. Reddy & K. Jamison (Eds.), *Team-building: Blueprints for productivity and satisfaction* (pp. 76-87). San Diego, CA: University Associates.

Hanson, P. G., & Lubin, B. (1989). Answers to questions frequently asked about organization development. In W. Sikes, A. Drexler, & J. Gant (Eds.), *The emerging practice of organization development* (pp. 15-23). San Diego, CA: University Associates.

Hanson, P. G., & Peck, C. P. (1974). Training for individual and group effectiveness and resourcefulness (TIGER). *Newsletter for Research in Mental Health and Behavioral Sciences* (Veterans Administration, Department of Medicine and Surgery), *16*(2), 1-3.

Hanson, P. G., Rothaus, P., Johnson, D. L., & Lyle, F. A. (1966). Autonomous groups in human relations training for psychiatric patients. *Journal of Applied Behavioral Science, 2*, 305-324.

Hanson, P. G., Rothaus, P., O'Connell, W. E., & Wiggins, G. (1969). Training patients for effective participation in back home groups. *American Journal of Psychiatry, 19*, 454-462.

Hanson, P. G., Rothaus, P., O'Connell, W. E., & Wiggins, G. (1970). Some basic concepts in human relations training for psychiatric patients. *Hospital and Community Psychiatry, 21*(5), 137-143.

Harrison, R. (in press). Strategy guidelines for an internal organization development unit. In R. Harrison (Ed.), *Collected papers of Roger Harrison*. San Francisco: Jossey-Bass.

Harvey, J. B. (1988). *The Abilene paradox*. Lexington, MA: D. C. Heath.

Heider, J. (1985). *The Tao of leadership*. New York: Bantam.

Herman, S. M. (1994). *The Tao at work: On leading and following*. San Francisco: Jossey-Bass.

Homans, G. C. (1950). *The human group*. New York: Harcourt, Brace.

Huczynski, A. (1987). *Encyclopedia of organizational change methods*. Hants, UK: Gower.

Hunt, D., & Hait, P. (1990). *The Tao of time*. New York: Simon & Schuster.

Jayaram, G. K. (1976). Open systems planning. In W. G. Bennis, K. D. Benne, R. Chin, & K. Cory (Eds.), *The planning of change* (3rd ed., pp. 275-283). New York: Holt, Rinehart & Winston.

Juran, J. M. (1988). *Juran on planning for quality.* New York: Free Press.

Juran, J. M. (1989). *Juran on leadership for quality.* New York: Free Press.

Keirsey, D., & Bates, M. (1984). *Please understand me: Character and temperament types.* Del Mar, CA: Prometheus.

Kroeger, O., & Thuesen, J. M. (1988). *Type talk: Or how to determine your personality type and change your life.* New York: Delacorte.

Lake, D. G., Miles, M. B., & Earle, R. B., Jr. (1973). *Measure human behavior.* New York: Teachers College Press.

Lau, J. B. (1975). *Behavior in organizations: An experiential approach.* Homewood, IL: Richard D. Irwin.

Leary, T. (1957). *Interpersonal diagnosis of personality.* New York: Ronald Press.

Levine, M. F., Taylor, J. C., & Davis, L. E. (1984). Defining quality of working life. *Human Relations, 37*(1), 81-104.

Lewin, K. (1935). *A dynamic theory of personality.* New York: McGraw-Hill.

Likert, R. (1967). *The human organization: Its management and value.* New York: McGraw-Hill.

Likert, R., & Likert, J. (1976). *New ways of managing conflict.* New York: McGraw-Hill.

Lippitt, J. R. (1959). Dimensions of the consultant's job. *Journal of Social Issues, 15*(2), 5-12.

Marrow, A. J. (1969). *The practical theorist: The life and work of Kurt Lewin.* New York: Basic Books.

McGregor, D. (1960). *The human side of enterprise.* New York: McGraw-Hill.

McLaughlin, C. P., & Kaluzny, A. D. (1990). Total quality management in health: Making it work. *Health Care Management Review, 15*(3), 7-14.

Messing, B. (1989). *The Tao of management.* Atlanta, GA: Humanics New Age.

Miller, F. A. (1994). Preface. In E. Y. Cross, J. H. Katz, F. A. Miller, & E. W. Seashore (Eds.), *The promise of diversity* (p. xxix). New York: Irwin.

Myers, I. B. (1980). *Gifts differing.* Palo Alto, CA: Consulting Psychologists Press.

Ouchi, W. G. (1981). *Theory Z.* Reading, MA: Addison-Wesley.

Ouchi, W. G., & Jaeger, A. (1978, April). Type Z organization: Stability in the midst of mobility. *Academy of Management Review,* pp. 305-314.

Pasmore, W. A., & Sherwood, J. J. (1978). Organizations as socio-technical systems. In W. A. Pasmore & J. J. Sherwood (Eds.), *Sociotechnical systems: A source book* (pp. 3-7). La Jolla, CA: University Associates.

Pasmore, W. A., & Sherwood, J. J. (1994). *Designing organizations that really work* [Brochure]. San Francisco: Organizational Consultants Inc.

Pfeiffer, J. W., Heslin, R., & Jones, J. E. (1976). *Instrumentation in human relations training.* San Diego: University Associates.

Reddy, B. W., & Jamison, K. (Eds.). (1988). *Team building: Blueprints for productivity and satisfaction.* San Diego, CA: University Associates.

Sashkin, M. (1984). A guide to participative management. *1984 Annual: Developing Human Resources* (pp. 227-240), San Deigo, CA: NTL Institute and University Associates.

Schein, E. H. (1985). *Organizational culture and leadership.* San Francisco: Jossey-Bass.

Schein, E. J. (1987). *Process consultation: Vol. 2. Lessons for managers and consultants.* Reading, MA: Addison-Wesley.

Schein, E. H. (1988). *Process consultation: Vol. 1. Its role in organization development.* Reading, MA: Addison-Wesley.

Schendel, D. E., & Hofer, C. W. (Eds.). (1979). *Strategic management.* Boston: Little, Brown.

Schmidt, W. H., & Finnegan, J. P. (1993). *TQManager: A practical guide for managing in a total quality organization.* San Francisco: Jossey-Bass.

Schmuck, R. A., & Miles, M. B. (Eds.). (1971). *Organization development in schools.* Palo Alto, CA: National Press.

Schutz, W. (1978). *FIRO awareness scales manual.* Palo Alto, CA: Consulting Psychologists Press.

Senge, P. M. (1990). *The fifth discipline: The art and practice of the learning organization.* New York: Doubleday.

Shani, A. B., & Elliott, O. (1989). Sociotechnical system design in transition. In W. Sikes, A. Drexler, & J. Gant (Eds.), *The emerging practice of organization development* (pp. 187-198). San Diego, CA: NTL Institute and University Associates.

Steele, F. (1973). *Physical settings and organization development.* Reading, MA: Addison-Wesley.

Summer, C. E. (1980). *Strategic behavior in business and government.* Boston: Little, Brown.

Trist, E. L. (1982). The sociotechnical perspective. In A. H. Van de Ven & W. F. Joyce (Eds.), *Perspectives on organization design and behavior* (pp. 19-75). New York: John Wiley.

Vaill, P. B. (1989a). *Managing as a performing art: New ideas for a world of chaotic change.* San Francisco: Jossey-Bass.

Vaill, P. B. (1989b). Seven process frontiers for organization development. In W. Sikes, A. Drexler, & J. Gant (Eds.), *The emerging practice of organization development* (pp. 261-272). San Diego, CA: NTL Institute and University Associates.

Walton, R. (1987). *Managing conflict: Interpersonal dialogue and third-party roles.* Reading, MA: Addison-Wesley.

Webster's New World Dictionary of American English. (1988). (3rd college ed.). New York: Simon & Schuster.

Weihrich, H. (1982). The TOWS matrix—a tool for situational analysis. *Long Range Planning, 15*(2), 54-66.

Weisbord, M. R. (1987). *Productive workplaces: Organizing and managing for dignity, meaning and community.* San Francisco: Jossey Bass.

Wheatley, M. J. (1992). *Leadership and the new science: Learning about organizations from an orderly universe.* San Francisco: Berrett-Koehler.

Yankelovich, D. (1981). New rules in American life: Searching for self-fulfillment in a world turned upside down. *Psychology Today, 15*(4), 35-91.

About the Authors

Philip G. Hanson, Ph.D., was Chief of the Psychology Service at Veterans Affairs (VA) Medical Center, Houston, Texas, for 4 years until his retirement in April 1989. During his 30-year career at the VA Medical Center, he was also Director of the Human Interaction Training Laboratory for hospitalized patients and the nationwide VA project "Training for Individual and Group Effectiveness and Resourcefulness" (TIGER). He is a certified and licensed psychologist in the state of Texas and is Clinical Professor, Department of Psychiatry and Behavioral Science, at the Baylor College of Medicine, Houston, Texas; and Research and Training Consultant to the VA Medical Center. He is a member of the National Training Laboratories Institute for Applied Behavioral Science (and was on the Board of Directors from 1978 to 1981); he is also a fellow of the American Psychological Association. He received the Professional Service Award from the Association of VA Chief Psychologists in 1981 and the Lifetime Achievement Award by the Houston Psychological Association in 1995. He has conducted workshops for and provided consultation to a variety of organizations in the areas of education, business, government, community, health care delivery systems, and religion, and has published three books and many articles in the field of small-group behavior and experiential learning.

Bernard Lubin, Ph.D., is Professor of Psychology and Administration at the University of Missouri at Kansas City, and former Chairperson of the Department of Psychology. He received his Ph.D. in psychology from Pennsylvania State University, and has been involved for a number of years in consulting, training, teaching, and research. His special areas of interest are the assessment and development of executives and managers and the development and renewal of organizations. He has conducted many workshops on interpersonal communication skills, group leadership skills, planning and problem solving, career planning, and developing subordinates. His extensive list of publications includes two volumes of organizational consultation case studies, and articles on team building, support systems in organizations, and the psychological impact of career disruptions. A partial list of his clients includes U.S. Sprint Corporation, NTL Institute, Eli Lilly Pharmaceutical Company, Panhandle Eastern Pipeline Company, Marion Merrill Dow, the American Nurses Association, and Standard-Havens Steel Company.